# RUFFIAN

A RACETRACK ROMANCE

# RUFFIAN

## A RACETRACK ROMANCE

William Nack

ISBN-13: 978-1-933060-30-9
ISBN-10: 1-933060-30-1

ESPN books are available for special promotions and premiums. For details
contact Michael Rentas, Assistant Director, Inventory Operations,
Hyperion, 77 West 66th Street, 11th floor, New York, New York 10023,
or call 212-456-0133.

FIRST EDITION

10 9 8 7 6 5 4 3 2 1

ESPN
BOOKS
a division of
ESPN publishing

# Ruffian's Pedigree

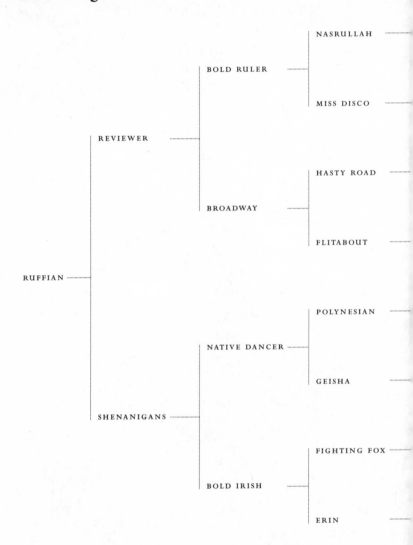

RUFFIAN
- REVIEWER
  - BOLD RULER
    - NASRULLAH
    - MISS DISCO
  - BROADWAY
    - HASTY ROAD
    - FLITABOUT
- SHENANIGANS
  - NATIVE DANCER
    - POLYNESIAN
    - GEISHA
  - BOLD IRISH
    - FIGHTING FOX
    - ERIN

| | | |
|---|---|---|
| NEARCO | PHAROS | |
| | NOGARA | |
| MUMTAZ BEGUM | BLENHEIM II | |
| | MUMTAZ MAHAL | THE TETRARCH |
| | | LADY JOSEPHINE |
| DISCOVERY | DISPLAY | |
| | ARIADNE | |
| OUTDONE | POMPEY | |
| | SWEEP OUT | |
| ROMAN | SIR GALLAHAD III | |
| | BUCKUP | |
| TRAFFIC COURT | DISCOVERY | |
| | TRAFFIC | |
| CHALLEDON | CHALLENGER II | |
| | LAURA GAL | |
| BIRD FLOWER | BLUE LARKSPUR | |
| | LA MOME | |
| UNBREAKABLE | SICKLE | |
| | BLUE GRASS | |
| BLACK POLLY | POLYMELIAN | |
| | BLACK QUEEN | |
| DISCOVERY | DISPLAY | |
| | ARIADNE | |
| MIYAKO | JOHN P. GRIER | |
| | LA CHICA | |
| SIR GALLAHAD III | TEDDY | |
| | PLUCKY LIEGE | |
| MARGUERITE | CELT | |
| | FAIRY RAY | |
| TRANSMUTE | BROOMSTICK | |
| | TRAVERSE | |
| ROSIE O'GRADY | HAMBURG | |
| | CHEROKEE ROSE II | |

*In our rhythm of earthly life we tire of light.*
*We are glad when the day ends, when the play ends;*
*and ecstasy is too much pain.*

— T.S. ELIOT

. . . . . . . . . . . . . . . . .

I N THE END, BEYOND ALL THE SCREAMS AND CRIES and the lifting of that ominous screen, at the center of all the clamor and the chaos and that scent of panic curling upward in the tremulous air, young Barbaro stood naked in the grandstand shade, his shoulder muscles quivering as he shifted on his three perfect feet. Gnawing on the bit between his teeth, his large eyes rolling white with panic, the bay raised and pumped the shattered remnant of his right rear leg, broken like a jigsaw puzzle in some thirty places. He touched the foot to the ground, raised it once more, and angrily punched the air.

Seeing this, I felt as though I'd been transported back in time again, doing it all over once again, running madly through the clubhouse and down the stairs two at a time, gulping sunlight as I stepped onto the Pimlico racetrack. Piddling along with my head down, I walked toward the stricken horse as if in sleep, fumbling and feeling my way along the damp walls of the same recurring nightmare that long ago I'd come to know so well, the one where Ruffian had come and gone in a thrash of dying light. Jamie Richardson, the track superintendent, was crouching under Barbaro and working to fit him with a temporary aluminum splint. A handful of racetrack workers stood on either side of the horse, trying to keep him calm while Richardson worked under him. Barbaro was in deepening pain as the flow of natural adrenaline began to wear off. He looked worried and confused. In his brief and simple life, he had always had four legs on which to stand and move and now for the first time he had only three, and he had never known such pain, and all of this and the excitement were arousing fear in his eyes. Barbaro lifted and cocked his injured leg, then flashed it just past Richardson's ear, missing it by inches.

"Watch it, dammit!" said a voice. "He'll kick your brains out."

"Whoa! Whoa, son," said Richardson.

"Easy with him," said a voice from the crowd.

"Oh jeez, oh jeez, please be careful with him," said another.

A man appeared carrying a walkie-talkie telephone. The crowd on the track grew larger. "Where's the doc?" the man said. "Get the X-ray machine to Barbaro's stall. Now! That's right. And make sure Doc Dreyfuss can get out on the track ... Who are all these people? Get these people off the track."

From the fans pressed against the nearby rail came a woman's voice: "Help him! Please help him."

Richardson was having trouble fitting on the cast. The colt kept moving the injured leg. "Whoa, son ... whoa," he said. "Hold him. Hold him."

More fans gathered behind the fence, faces hung as in a still-life watercolor, hands on lips, fingers on cheeks, women in tears. "Don't kill him," one said. "Please, please don't kill him!"

She had seen the screen, the one they always raise to protect the people from their feelings, to block the view of crowds when they have to destroy hopelessly injured animals through lethal injection, and Barbaro looked wild-eyed when he saw the large screen looming towards him. The horse's trainer, Michael Matz, shouted, "Get that screen out of here! You're scaring the horse."

The cast was on and the ambulance door opened. "We're ready to load," said a member of the ambulance crew. "Get the horse turned around."

Barbaro hobbled onto the back of the van and left to a flutter of cheers.

It was May 20, 2006, 6:35 p.m., and one of the hoariest of racetrack rituals had just played out on a national stage before an audience repelled and mesmerized by the drama. The horses had just finished racing across the finish line in the 131st running of the Preakness Stakes at Pimlico, the second leg of racing's Triple Crown. This was not the way it was supposed to end, not for the newest rising star of the sport. Two weeks earlier, the undefeated Barbaro had won the Kentucky Derby with a verve and panache not often seen at Churchill Downs, and he had come to the Preakness looking and acting like a horse whose destiny was writ by the wind that gusted at his back— like a horse certain to become the first Triple Crown winner in twenty-eight years, since Affirmed won the Belmont and swept the Crown in 1978. It all ended before Barbaro had traveled two hundred yards, the instant when the hind leg broke and kept breaking and shattering in smaller and smaller shards as he struggled to run on … until Edgar Prado, sawing frantically on the lines, finally reined him to a stop.

So there was Richardson fumbling to fit the cast and the silent arrival of the horse ambulance and the raising of the screen, all those pinched and melancholy faces circling the animal. More vivid than that was how the scene so eerily conjured the past, sending me back to that airless afternoon thirty-one years earlier at Belmont Park when Ruffian, the flying black filly, broke down six hundred yards into her match race with Kentucky Derby winner Foolish Pleasure, and I took off through the clubhouse and raced down the stairs and swept blindly past a guard and onto the crown of the track, where I heard a jockey screaming at me just before his muscular bay colt thundered past, nearly bowling me over as he came home alone in triumph past the finish line. I ran across the infield to where she had broken down and there he was, the man crouching under her, fumbling with the cast. Saw the ambulance rolling to a stop and saw the lifting of the screen as the filly stood there trembling and wide-eyed and scared, sweat pouring off her in the heat of that early Sunday evening: July 6, 1975. Went unwelcome to her burial at dusk the next night, on the infield at Belmont Park, and stood outside the small urn of light cast by the headlights from the truck that had borne her enshrouded remains from Doc Reed's hospital across the road.

Undefeated in ten starts, in front at every pole in every race in which she ever ran, Ruffian was more than just another transient champion passing through. She was of a certain singularity that hinted of origins almost divine. Even today, more than three decades later, I can still close my eyes and see her out there running on the lead, always on the lead, her black silhouette in full flight, free running as a child on a playground, five lengths in front, her clipped mane swept back and her tail rippling like a little flag, her swan's neck rising and dipping to the tom-tom beating of her hooves, nine in front and widening, her jockey sitting quiet as a piece of marble statuary on her long back, his little hands motionless, his body rocking wavelike to the hitchless rhythms of her stride, the filly pricking her ears forward and picking up the tempo once again, now fourteen in front and coasting, everything so effortless, the jockey's silks billowing along his shoulders and back, now fifteen in front, expanding toward us on the turn for home, sailing into our lives and our history as if upon an upward draft of wind.

Ruffian was a portrait of grace illumined by an inner fire. Not only was she the fastest filly in the modern history of the American turf, but she most certainly ranks among the fastest two-year-olds who ever lived, male or female, gray or bay, in the Old World or the New. Ruffian was America's homegrown version of her own most celebrated ancestress, the Aga Khan's legendary Mumtaz Mahal, England's so-called Flying

Filly, a gray bullet who is widely remembered for being among the very fastest two-year-olds of all time and who undoubtedly derived most of her unearthly speed from her sire, a sensation of the species named The Tetrarch—he who wore that oddly speckled gray coat, he who was known throughout the British Isles as the Spotted Wonder, he who had so little interest in sex that he sired only 130 foals in his abbreviated career at stud, preferring rather to stop and gaze at birds strutting on a rooftop as he headed for a tryst with a hot mare in the breeding shed. The Tetrarch may have been equinely gay, but he did leave one luminous, enduring mark upon the thoroughbred breed. Led to the court of the Lady Josephine, a comely golden chestnut with two white stockings and fiery turn of foot herself, The Tetrarch did not pause to watch the birds. Eleven months later, in the spring of 1921, the Lady dropped Mumtaz Mahal. In one deft roll of his genetic dice, the Spotted Wonder thus begat the only two-year-old in English turf history who may have been as fast as he. More importantly, through the last fifty years of the 20th Century, and even through the first decade of the 21st, the Flying Filly's influence and power as a broodmare has continued to blow through the ancestral trees of thoroughbreds around the world, of champion after champion, from Secretariat to Northern Dancer to Seattle Slew, touching even the branch of Barbaro. But it was not until 1974—on May 22, at Belmont Park, in an otherwise unimportant maiden race for two-year-old fillies—that The Tetrarch's long-dead flying daughter was truly born again, her blazing speed incarnated in another.

. . . . . . . . . . . . . . . . .

I have thought of Ruffian so often over the years that today she flits around like a ghost in all the mustier rooms of my reveries, a boarder who has had a run of the place the last two years, still appearing most insistently during my periodic visits to

Belmont Park on Long Island, that mammoth 1½-mile bridle path where she lived most of her racetrack life and where she raced and trained and grew in size and stature. This was where I often saw her as she walked of early mornings to and from her fast works and long gallops, her bespectacled trainer, Frank Y. Whiteley, leading her on his pony to the track, loose-reining him under that signature straw fedora, a cigarette cupped in his hand, now and then turning in the saddle to watch her walk or share a word with her rider, either jockey Jacinto Vasquez or exercise boy Yates Kennedy. In the last year or so, particularly, Ruffian had seemed everywhere I turned.

A month before Barbaro limped to the outer rail at old Pimlico, I was working on a movie set at Belmont Park, consulting on a dramatic film about Ruffian's life, and by the last day of the shoot I felt as though I were drifting in and out of different eras, slip-sliding through time zones, here one minute and gone again, living once more through the summers of '74 and '75, seeing it and feeling it as I had never thought it possible to do. The Hollywood illusionists, at work like trolls, had created a world in restoration. All the cars were restored from the early 1970s and the extras were attired in the suede and polyesters common back then, even wearing period wrist-watches and eyeglasses, and soon I was beginning to have trouble separating Sam Shepard, the award-winning playwright turned actor, from Frank Whiteley, the trainer. Sam was looking and acting more like Whiteley every day. He had Frank measured all right, down to the hat and glasses and the way he talked and moved. Sam had even begun to fool himself. One afternoon in the walking ring at Belmont Park, as they were preparing to shoot a scene that would depict Shepard entering the paddock with one of the Ruffian stand-ins, director Yves Simoneau was staring into a video monitor and watching an old clip of Whiteley leading Ruffian into that very same paddock thirty-one years ago when Shepard, joining Simoneau, said, "Hey, that's pretty good. When did we shoot that scene?"

"Sam, this is real footage," Yves said. "That's the real Frank—the real Ruffian."

They shot the burial scene the final day. They had dug a large five-foot-deep hole in the Belmont infield and lowered into it a large cardboard figure of a horse whose body had been wrapped in a white tarp that one of the crew had picked up in the paint department of a Home Depot down the road.

I peered into the hole in the ground, wavering momentarily, feeling lost in the brown abyss. "Is that how she looked when they brought her over?" Simoneau asked me.

Thinking back, I conjured up the grainy memories of that faraway night. "It was dark when they brought her over and all I could see was a horse's body wrapped in a piece of white cloth," I said. "Silence, headlights, broken shadows … "

"Like this?" Yves asked.

I looked down into the hole again. "Yeah, yeah," I said. "A horse in a white shroud. This is how I remember her looking that night."

I needed to get away from this; the whole scene was beginning to unnerve me: the faux grave, Mnemosyne's Trojan horse dressed like a window manikin, the crew and actors standing solemnly around that cavity in the earth, the probing one-eyed lenses grinding away, the imaginative flights of fakery, the peeling back of skin, the stillness of the moment, the real memories of that long run across the infield in the wavering heat.

"You been to Ruffian's grave site yet?" I had asked Shepard.

"I went over there earlier," he said. "I stayed quite a while. Very impressive headstone."

So I drifted down the inner rail of the turf course, to the flagpole rising not far from a pond of geese, to the headstone encircled by shrubbery shaped like a horse-shoe. I stood reading from the marker in the fleeting afternoon light.

### Ruffian
### Undefeated two-year-old Filly Champion of 1974

And then the names of all the big stakes that she had won: the Fashion ... the Astoria ... the Sorority ... the Spinaway ... the Triple Crown for three-year-old fillies at Belmont: the Acorn ... the Mother Goose ... the Coaching Club American Oaks. I crossed the infield and came to the fence along the backstretch where the pigeons, pecking at undigested kernels of oats dropped in the manure, had heard the colt and the filly hurtling towards them on the backstretch and burst upward in a flutter of wings, ten feet in the air and rising, as startled as flushed quails, and at that instant in July, thirty-one years ago, her world began to come apart, in splinters. So I turned and looked at the grandstand six hundred yards away and saw Ruffian flashing off the turn for home in the Fashion or the Acorn—all her races looked so much alike—Vasquez leaning back with a long hold as she loped into the bridle on cruise control. I saw the way she came to the paddock for the Astoria, so clearly up to no good, moving into the walking ring as through a lobby bar, like some willowy hooker on the make, that black satin dress pulled tight around her full and nearly perfect derriere. And I saw her brilliant final quarter in the Spinaway Stakes at Saratoga that cloudy August afternoon, echoes from the ancient reaches of her pedigree, and heard and felt the electric exuberance of the clubhouse crowds, all those fancy breeders and owners, as it crackled like a blue spark up and down the rows of iron girders and the box seats.

Over there was LeRoy Jolley, the trainer of Foolish Pleasure, staring intently at Ruffian from that box seat at Belmont as she sped by him in the Oaks, on her way to the match race, and there was the way she showed up at Aqueduct the first time she ran at age three, turning the post parade into a kind of beauty pageant, looking more like a show horse than the thoroughbred that she was.

And let's see ... there was the first time that I'd ever heard her name, in that surprising telephone call that came the evening of May 22, 1974, as I labored to finish my biography of Secretariat, the 1973 Triple Crown winner. The caller was *Newsday* handicapper John Pricci, my friend and newspaper colleague, who had turned to a life of playing the horses and analyzing the races when his dreams of being a nightclub singer died in tone-deaf Queens. John rarely called me at home, but he had something to sing about that night.

"You remember Icecapade?" he asked.

"A gray horse, a very fast miler," I said. "Wrote about him once, I think, when he won the Stuyvesant Handicap. Brilliant. Very well-bred. By Nearctic out of Shenanigans. The Whiteleys had her. David Whiteley, I think. Maybe Frank. Why? Did he die or something?"

Pricci laughed. "No, no," he said. "I saw his half sister today, a two-year-old filly, in her first race. She wins by fifteen and ties the track record! *In hand!* Goin' five and a half furlongs. I'm just callin' to say you *gotta* see this filly!"

"What's her name?"

"Ruffian … "

"Ruffian? Sounds like a colt."

"She ain't no colt," John said. "She's a freak. Unbelievable. I mean, when's the last time you saw a two-year-old filly win by fifteen in her first start and equal the track record? *Any* two-year-old?"

"How fast she go?"

"Would you believe one-oh-three flat?" he said. A minute and three seconds.

"Who's she by?"

"Reviewer. Remember him? One of those Phipps homebreds by Bold Ruler."

I knew Reviewer all right. He could hum. Bold Ruler was among the greatest sires of the 20th century, an extremely fast racehorse who imparted his crackling speed to many of his progeny. Secretariat was by far the greatest of Bold Ruler's many sons, a horse who could win from the sprints to the classic distances and beyond, and Reviewer was perceived as the second fastest horse the stallion ever sired—a horse who was endowed with world-class lick but whose career as a runner had been plagued by problems of unsoundness not unknown to branches of his mother's tribe. Soft boned, Reviewer had suffered three physical breakdowns during his career and started only thirteen times in three years, winning nine, before they packed him off to stud at Claiborne Farm. There the usual bovine herd of Kentucky breeders, fairly drooling over a pedigree laced with the most coveted of all qualities—the gene in which came bottled that mystical genie of speed—would line up and give him ample opportunities to pass along both his surpassing athleticism and his Wedgwood fragility, until he broke down one day in 1977, while running in his paddock at Claiborne Farm, and two weeks later had to be destroyed.

The memory is vague but I think I saw Reviewer set a track record in the Nassau County Handicap at Belmont Park in 1970, nine furlongs in 1:46⅘, but all I can remember now is how homely he looked in the post parade, his Roman-nosed Bold Ruler head shaped like a brown jug. Oh, but how that beast could run!

"What does she look like?" I asked.

"She's big, she's black, and she's beautiful," John said. "What can I tell ya? You gotta see this filly to believe it. That's all anybody could talk about. The place was, like, giddy. She goes to the lead out of the gate and opens five and then eight and ten and then fifteen. Vasquez never moved on her. *Easy!*"

It was growing late. I was beginning to feel anxious, vulnerable, edgy. I was mired in the middle of writing about Secretariat's epochal thirty-one-length victory in the Belmont Stakes eleven months before, the greatest performance in the history of the sport by the most brilliant racehorse in history, and now the old crooner was telling me that a gorgeous black freak had emerged at Belmont Park, a rival to my hero, this fur coat draped in oyster pearls, and as insane and irrational as this may sound, I sensed at once this veil of resentment coming over me, of something quite as palpable as jealousy, and that disagreeable sensation did not begin to lift until I finally laid eyes on her, at that moment when she glided into the Belmont paddock for the Fashion Stakes, in the second start of her life, and even then it never wholly went away until the night of the burial on the Belmont infield, where you could see the jiggling headlights of the ambulance as it curved around the little lake and slowed as it approached the small band of mourners who had gathered around the grave, waiting for her there in silent grief.

.................

I was Chicago-born, in a hospital not far from the great ivied haunt of Wrigley Field, but my parents soon joined the great post-War migration out of the city and we settled in Skokie, a village to the north, in '51. My sister Dee and I soon began mucking the stalls and grooming the inhabitants of a riding stable in nearby Morton Grove. We took aging livery horses down cindered riding trails that wended through the surrounding forests; by 1955, we had our own charger, a parade horse born with an all-white body and a mask-like black head that Dee called fittingly The Bandit, and I was riding in horse shows and passing my teens in the company of the world's fanciest gaited saddle horses, from the legendary and undefeated Wing Commander to Bo Jangles, whose colored photos faced each other for years on my bedroom wall. They were hung in honor of that night in December 1955 when I saw the twelve-year-old Wing Commander's final performance in that crumbling old amphitheater down by the Chicago stockyards; he and Bo Jangles went at each other in that hot arena minute by mounting minute and whip over spur, chillingly through the slow gait and

Swaps with trainer Mesh Tenney

the trot, until finally the crowds came bolting to their feet as the mane-flying Commander racked furiously past, his muscular legs pumping him right into history as the greatest five-gaited saddle horse of all time. The howls still sing in my ears.

This may not have been clear to me then, but the Commander's ringing farewell to that world echoed my own goodbye to all that. As surpassingly lovely a creature as Wing Commander was, both in physique and in motion, he and his breed had already lost their emotional hold on me the summer before, on the afternoon I was hanging over the rail at Washington Park and this golden chestnut came walking past. He stopped in front of me and dropped his nose over the fence as if to say, "How do you do?" This was Swaps—three months after his Kentucky Derby victory over Nashua and just a week away from his rendezvous with Traffic Judge, one of his talented coevals, in the $100,000 American Derby. His rider, Bill Shoemaker, was on him. It was between races, and he and Bill were out for a stroll in the afternoon sun.

The horse I see in memory now looks tall and radiant. Swaps had a large, luminous brown eye, an exquisitely Aegean head and face that looked chiseled in cameo, and a warm, friendly breath that he held for a moment as your offered hand, cupped downward, rose and drew near him.

"You can touch him, he won't bite," said the Shoe. "He's very kind."

The horse sniffed the hand and settled, dropping his head for a pat. His jowl was large and soft. His demeanor was calm and poised. The Shoe nudged the rein and they turned and left. I was all of fourteen years and six months old, but that horse did own a piece of me from that hour on. A week later there he was again at old Washington Park, lunging through the homestretch like a panther in the gloaming, three in front, his powerful shoulders glinting in the light as he reached his forelegs far in front of him and galloped home in hand, beating Traffic Judge with ease and setting a new course record of $1:54\frac{3}{5}$.

He was magnificent. My dad rolled a stogie between his teeth, working his eyebrows like Groucho, up-down-up-down, as Swaps galloped under the wire. Turning to my mother, he said, "Wow! What a horse!"

That was all a young boy needed to hear. The clarity of that performance, the decisive finality that I had yearned for and missed in the world of horse shows ruled by fallible and sometimes idiotic judges, had won me to racing as a sport and to the memory of that horse forever. Eleven days after the American Derby, Swaps and Nashua met at Washington Park for the greatest match race run in America since Seabiscuit beat War Admiral at Pimlico in 1938. It was a national television spectacle, a mile and a quarter at full bore, and hundreds of turf writers from around the world descended on Chicago to cover it. The match race was on Wednesday and my father was at work, so I sat at home to suffer it in silence on a fifteen-inch Admiral television set. There were rumors all week that Swaps had had a recurrence of an old foot injury—it was oozing pus and he was lame on the morning of the race—but such news was of no solace after the two colts broke with a fury out of the gate and Eddie Arcaro on Nashua, racing on the inside, forced Swaps to the outside on the first turn, to the deeper, muddier, more tiring part of the track, prompted a blistering pace all the way around and then pulled away in the stretch, with Swaps physically wavering on that sore foot, to win by 6½ lengths.

I burst out the front door of the house, got sick on a neighbor's front yard tree, and then rode around the village for the next two hours, in an unfamiliar state akin to grief. This was not about the hapless, if beloved, Cubs dropping another two at Wrigley. This was not about the Go-Go White Sox failing again. This was not even about the Brooklyn Dodgers, our surrogate World Series team, losing yet another to the Yankees. This was a far more crushing blow and it had as much to do with loyalty and love as it had to do with pride and loss. That week, I found a photo of Swaps' patrician head in a magazine; in an act of defiant loyalty, the bitter defeat be damned, I cut it out and slipped it into the first of a dozen or so wallets I would own over the years: so many years and wallets that, in 1965, I had the photo undergo an emergency lamination in order to save it from disintegrating entirely—until, alas, the last swatch of genuine leather was lifted from me in Madison Square Garden before a fight I was covering between Roberto Duran and Davey Moore, on June 16, 1983, and I never saw it again.

What I did bring with me from that darksome day in August, what was not picked from that pocket, was a deeply ingrained suspicion of match races and anxiety over the unseemly pressures of their invariably hot and insane pace, and beyond that the fears of loss and heartbreak that attended them.

Over the next twenty years, though I lived and moved in many guises, in foreign lands from Mexico to Southeast Asia to Japan, I never strayed too long or far from the runners and the racetracks of the world. They were my relief, my anodyne, the only traceable threads in my otherwise tangled web of memories, a fertile source and structure for the richest and wildest of my fantasies: striding into flower-bedecked winner's circles at Churchill Downs, Pimlico and Belmont Park, my fists pumping to salute the cheers of the multitudes as my homebred chestnut, nostrils flared, gallops to victory in the Triple Crown ... poring in candlelight over the pedigrees of leading stallions in America and England, looking for the right genetic nick for my fifteen blue-hen broodmares ... greeting a half-dozen desert sheikhs as they arrive in Gulfstream jets with portmanteaus sardined with stacks of $100 bills, offering to buy my champion two-year-old for $50 million cash ... flying my unbeaten Triple Crown champion to the world's greatest horse race, the Prix de l'Arc de Triomphe at Longchamp, in Paris, and basking in his reflected glory as he wins in a romp by five, then dining that night off the Champs-Elysées, where I buy a first edition of *Le Monde* and see that he is feted as the fastest horse in history … and then dancing till first light in the Garden of Tuileries.

I had seen very early, in horses from Native Dancer to Swaps to Round Table, the poetry that had inspired the ancient Bedouin legend writ in the sand: "And God took a handful of southerly wind, blew his breath over it, and created the horse." And I would see in my father's jubilant face, whenever he saw a Swaps or a Round Table galloping free to the wire, a confirmation of that likable Winston Churchill aphorism: "There is something about the outside of a horse that is good for the inside of a man."

So I kind of made a life with horses wherever I went—as a groom at the big Chicago tracks in the summer of '59, where I fed and rubbed four horses and took one to the paddock, a filly named Queen of Turf, and watched her win by three; as a closet student of racing history and lore at the University of Illinois' main library, where I used to steal away to the underground stacks and mix readings of Milton and Mill with obscure texts on 19th century pedigrees and *The Influence of Desert Warrior Horses on the Modern Thoroughbred*; and as a young infantry lieutenant driving with my pregnant wife, Mary, south from Illinois to Fort Benning, Georgia, by way of the Blue Grass, where my tortuous search ended by a paddock rail at Darby Dan Farm when that comely chestnut stallion, the one with the head and ears sculpted by Praxiteles, saw us from a distance and strode over, dropping his nose over the rail.

"He won't bite you," I said. "He's very kind."

"How do you know?" she said.

"I met him once."

"You met him?" She made a face. "Who introduced you?"

"Bill Shoemaker."

"Who is *he*?" she asked.

She fed the horse some jelly beans and he lowered his head further and nuzzled her swollen belly. Swaps had gotten huskier in the ten years since I'd last seen him at work in Chicago, a year after the match with Nashua, the week he came sailing home at some 40 miles an hour, with his ears pricked, in the Washington Park Handicap, nearly smashing his own world record for the mile. He broke four world time records in 1956, along with two other track records, in the greatest exhibition of speed in the history of the turf. I told my wife how he had won the Kentucky Derby and lost the match race and how his finest son, Chateaugay, the big young stallion in the adjoining paddock, had done his daddy proud and won the Derby in '63. Here I took the laminated photo out of my wallet and showed it to her.

"Why do you have that picture in your wallet?"

"I like his face," I said.

.................

Twenty-two months later I was hunkered down at Tan Son Nhut Air Base outside Saigon, lying on the floor of my bullet-scarred office during the Tet Offensive of '68, watching Cobra gunships rocket and rake with Gatling guns the little cemetery that lay beyond the barbed wire fence of MACV headquarters. I stared for hours at the nightlong descent of burning flares that clustered and hung like a chandelier of candles from the dome of the Tonkin sky, all the while listening to the audiotapes of race calls that my mother had taken off radio and television broadcasts and had been sending to me faithfully for nearly a year. Not even the rat-a-tat-tat of machine guns or the distant thump of mortars could spoil the beauty, so vividly imagined in one hot and fetid room, of the gifted Damascus as he romped to his twenty-two-length triumph in the historic Travers Stakes at Saratoga in August of '67, or the mighty Dr. Fager's flight to victory in that summer's Arlington Classic, or Buckpasser's doggedly determined victory in the Suburban Handicap. That team of highborn steeds had pulled me as in a magic carriage through the length and loneliness of the war—into a fantastic world that I had come to know and cherish since I was a boy, a world painted in jockey silks and vibrant with the sound of flying hooves, a place redolent of mustard stands and oat mash cooking in feed tubs and of hot doughnuts and coffee at 5 a.m., of delicious liniments and unguents and of blue smoke curling from my father's cigars.

And five months after that, when I was the new Islip Town beat reporter at *Newsday*, looking for malfeasance at the local dump, my dad came to visit and we did something that we'd always talked of doing back when we were prowling the grandstands together at the great wooden bandboxes of Arlington and Washington parks. On July 20, 1968, we made the pilgrimage to what we'd always viewed, in our Midwestern provincialism, as the mythical kingdom of Aqueduct, the Big A. As we stood at the grandstand fence by the eighth pole, suddenly there they were, my two faithful companions from those lost days and nights in Southeast Asia, parading to the post for the 1¼-mile Brooklyn Handicap, both looking on the muscle, no longer figments of my black-and-white imagination but materializing there before me in seaside reds and browns, in sepia flesh: Damascus and Dr. Fager. I loved Damascus that day. The Big D looked splendid in the Big A paddock and he had his fleet-footed rabbit, Hedevar, there to force a fiery early pace and weaken the headstrong Dr. Fager; I nearly got into a row with two simian horseplayers who had bet their lungs on Dr. Fager when I told them the race set up better for Damascus, flashed the $100 win ticket that my dad had bet on him, and howled encouragement to his jockey, Manny Ycaza, through a series of sharp, high-pitched constrictions of the larynx that came out:

"Crush him, Manny! Wait 'til the last turn and run that big giraffe down!"

This is precisely how the Big D pulled it off. The final quarter-mile of that

Brooklyn Handicap was among the great glories of the American turf. By the quarter pole, Hedevar had done his trench work very well, running right alongside Dr. Fager and prompting him in a blistering early pace, the while Hedevar's jockey howled like a banshee in Dr. Fager's ear. His blood up, the good doctor grew increasingly rank and restless over the efforts of his rider, Braulio Baeza, to restrain him. By the turn for home, a weary Hedevar was hailing a cab, but Dr. Fager was beginning to melt around the wick of his own ardent pace. Ycaza saw this and he popped the question to Damascus. Instantly, like a big cat leaping from a tree, the Big D pounced, bounding to Dr. Fager's throat and wringing it there for all to see. Damascus flew past him off the final turn. He ran away with it to win by three, setting a track record for a mile and a quarter: 1:59⅕! My dad did a Fred Astaire to the windows to collect. Somewhere Churchill was smiling.

We had no way of knowing this then, no way anyone could know, but we had just begun to witness the dawning of the golden age of thoroughbred racing in America— a twelve-year stretch that saw the ascent of three Triple Crown winners, a raft of brilliant grass horses, sprinters and weight carriers, and some of the swiftest female runners of all time. Out of this veritable herd of talent, which began with Dark Mirage, the Big D and Dr. Fager and ended, in 1980, with Spectacular Bid, Genuine Risk and the coming of John Henry, the two most effulgent luminaries were Secretariat and Ruffian. And it was only by one extraordinary whorl of chance, a moment twisted by the bourbon in the eggnog, that I had a front row box to watch the whole glorious show. By mid-December of 1971, I had become *Newsday*'s resident expert in freshwater aquifers and sewers, in all their malodorous manifestations. I could discourse eloquently on secondary and tertiary treatment of sewage. I entertained whole dinner parties on the miracles of phosphorous and nitrogen removal, on the evils of septic tanks and saltwater intrusion. I drank with limnologists. Owl-eyed

Secretariat's historic
Belmont stretch run

conservationists called me at wee hours. I became a wastewater raconteur. I flew a bumper sticker that read "Save the Wetlands." I had spent my university years assidu-ously preparing myself to be a Latin America correspondent, studying the history and culture of the region and learning to speak fluent Spanish, but the closest I had come to Chapultepec Park was Pepe's Big Burrito in Queens.

And then, alas, at the perfect intersection of time and space, just as the only other world I really cared about was turning towards the sun, the fates intervened for me in ways never really expected. Late at the *Newsday* Christmas party with all of us far gone into the nog, I mounted the desk in the middle of the city room and summoned from memory the names of all ninety-seven Kentucky Derby winners—year by year—from Aristides' inaugural victory in 1875 to Canonero II's in 1971. I dismounted the table to boozy ripples of applause. The editor of *Newsday*, Dave Laventhol, at once sidled up next to me and asked, "Why do you know that?" I told him that racing was my passion, and I had memorized those names years before—the week after Swaps had run a mile in a blazing 1:33²/₅ in the 1956 Washington Park Handicap, a clocking that was only a fifth of a second off his own world record set that earlier summer. Laventhol knew I was restless and wanting to move on.

"Would you like to cover horse racing for us?" he asked. I thought I hadn't heard him right and I leaned in. "Seriously," he said. "We're adding a Sunday paper in the spring and we'll need someone to write about racing. It would be the perfect job for you."

Five minutes later, I accepted the job.

I felt like Papillon as he leapt off that cliff.

Jupiter was just beginning to align with Mars. On April 10, 1972, a month after I first walked into that stable area at Belmont Park, a copper-colored two-year-old who had just arrived from Hialeah Race Course in Florida, a colt untested and unknown, worked for the first time in his life at Belmont Park, breezing a half-mile in

:36²/₅ and his name was Secretariat. Seven days later, on April 17, at Claiborne Farm in Kentucky, Shenanigans dropped her foal by Reviewer. They called her Ruffian. No horse in modern times would rise higher and faster and larger than Secretariat in 1972 and 1973, culminating in his record-shattering Triple Crown, when his mug appeared on the front of three national newsmagazines in one week—*Time, Sports Illustrated* and *Newsweek*—and now I was nearly finished telling that tale when John Pricci called to say that this whole new comet had just sailed into our ken at Belmont Park. And then he called a second time.

"Remember that filly I was telling you about, Ruffian? She's in Wednesday. The Fashion Stakes."

. . . . . . . . . . . . . . . . .

Late in the afternoon of June 12, as horsemen and horseplayers leaned against the rails that rim the paddock at Belmont Park, as more came bounding through the glass doors behind the mammoth rear facade of racing's Taj Mahal, Ruffian traveled down the undulating walking path leading through the tunnel from the barns to the paddock. She emerged suddenly in front of the saddling stalls and stopped a moment to look at the crowds. They had come to see her and a one-eyed filly named Copernica, a daughter of the English champion Nijinsky II, have at each other in the 5½-furlong Fashion, an historic New York race that had been run since 1897 and had been won by some of the fastest tomboys in the history of the turf, from Top Flight and Bewitch to Affectionately and Rosie O'Grady. The same nimble-footed Rosie who later achieved even more lasting glory as a thoroughbred matriarch—an immortal producer whose enormously talented and sprawling family of children, grandchildren and beyond would number among them such leading lights as High Voltage and Intent,

Bewitch and Majestic Light, Stupendous and Impressive and … yes, the filly who had just made her appearance in the Belmont paddock. To trace a female line so rich in champions and gifted runners always calls to mind the old saying among breeders to describe such prolificacy: "There's an awful lot of trout in that stream." So it was with Rosie O'Grady, winner of the 1917 Fashion, who was Ruffian's maternal great-great-grandmother, for it was Rosie who dropped Erin, who dropped Bold Irish, who dropped Shenanigans, who dropped Ruffian.

None of these had ever made an entrance so grand as Ruffian's in the Fashion that day. Copernica was undefeated in two races and may have been a fan favorite, out of sympathy for her blind eye, but it was Ruffian who was drawing the crowds and causing the murmurous stir among them as trainer Frank Whiteley escorted her into the paddock. First thing I remember seeing was that little white snip between her eyes, almost a star, as she walked towards us past the saddling stalls. She looked quite elegant and lovely in the way she carried herself, so calm and restrained yet curious and alert, all the while acting sort of shy, like a teenage girl stepping on a dance floor for the first time. Nor is this first impression meant to convey in any way that she was gangly or awkward or afraid, but rather simply diffident as she looked down upon the humans milling around her. Tall as she was, she viewed the world with a decidedly regal air, owning a fine head, neat ears, and an extremely attractive face, all of which turned on her long, perfectly shaped and tapered neck. She was the Audrey Hepburn of her tribe, at least from the withers up, for she was also possessed of a magnificent racehorse body, especially for a filly so young—a body striking in the breadth of the shoulders and the musculature of the legs and hindquarters, which were unusually well-developed but not thickly bunched or in any way excessive; indeed, from head to foot, she had rather the long, leggy look of a horse built for the classic distances, a mile and a quarter or more. I was in the walking ring, moving towards her for an even closer look, when I heard a familiar voice, its nasally tuned French-Canadian accent rising from the shadow of the giant white pine just behind me: "Let me tell you, as God is my witness!"

It was Lucien Laurin, the trainer of Secretariat, being his irrepressibly expressive self. He was beaming at the filly as he had once beamed at the red horse now retired. "Look at the size of her!" Lucien said. "Christ almighty, look at that!"

Whiteley let Ruffian make a turn of the paddock, Vasquez perched upon her back, and we all tracked her as the field of six fillies filed out of the tunnel to the main oval. Ruffian's breeder and owner, Stuart Janney, sat down with Whiteley in the box seats. The place was buzzing with anticipation, and not only for the way she looked in the post parade, but also for the morning speed she had been flashing since she demolished that field of maidens by fifteen lengths in track record time. Just the morning before, on Tuesday, Frank sent her out for a final work, one designed to sharpen her speed, and she blazed through one of the fastest morning moves ever seen on the main track at Belmont Park, running an opening quarter-mile in :21³/₅ and three-eighths in a blistering :33 flat. I loved the clocker's droll humor in the *Daily Racing Form*: "Ruffian was full of run." Full of run, indeed! On March 14, 1973, I had seen Secretariat scorch over that same distance on that same track in :32³/₅, the fastest three-furlong work I have ever witnessed, but he was a strapping three-year-old by then, only seven weeks away from the Kentucky Derby, and here was this two-year-old filly—this baby, really—barreling around Breakfast at Belmont in a way that fairly took our breath away.

Poor little Copernica never saw her coming. Ruffian broke alertly, got herself together in the first one hundred yards, sailed to the front before she'd gone two hundred yards, then poured it on and on and on, racing the fastest opening half-mile run by any horse at Belmont that day, :45⅕. She cavalierly turned away Copernica's feeble challenge on the turn, this after Vasquez had sensed he was being followed. He had glanced around but he saw nothing. "I heard a noise behind me," he said. Ever so subtly he moved his hands, a signal Ruffian felt through the reins, and at once she picked up the beat on the turn for home, running away from Copernica through the lane and winning all alone by nearly seven. All clocks stopped at 1:03 flat. It was the second time in three weeks that she had tied the track record for the distance, her first victory in a stakes, and I wrote at the time: "Ruffian galloped back to the winner's circle at Belmont Park here yesterday with her breath coming deep and fast and her eyes as round as the globes on the furlong pole, about as wide as the eyes of Jacinto Vasquez, who was riding her."

Stuart Janney, a dignified and gray-haired gent of fifty-seven, the faintest of smiles on his handsome face, approached Vasquez in the circle as the jock slid off her back.

"She run pretty good, hey?" Mr. Janney said.

"Yes, sir," said Vasquez. "Very good … "

Now, looking quizzically at Vasquez, the Maryland breeder said, "Did you hit her *at all*?"

"Nahhhh!" said Vasquez, brushing the question aside. "There was nothing to it."

Frank took off for the barn, tracking Ruffian as she headed home around the paddock, and Vasquez was walking quickly towards the jockey's quarters when he ran into David Whiteley, Frank's son and assistant, and a respected horseman himself.

"*I* could have ridden her!" David kidded.

"That's sure," said Vasquez. The two were shaking hands when a jockey's valet, carrying a saddle, swept past them. "That's a Rolls-Royce!" he yelled to Jacinto.

Vasquez turned towards the valet and shrugged as the man ran down the stairs to the jock's room. "What did I tell you last week about this filly?" he yelled.

That I-told-you-so patina of swagger was quintessential Vasquez. He grew up on a little farm in Panama, one of ten kids, and ran away from home when still a boy to become a race rider. His was a hardscrabble existence, but he survived by his wits and talent and came to the United States in 1960 with the hope of emulating his hero, fellow Panamanian Braulio Baeza, then on a fast march to becoming one of America's greatest riders. By the time I met him, in 1972, Vasquez was on the rising crest of a career that would sweep him to two victories in the Kentucky Derby, to a staggering 5,231 wins, and a place in the National Racing Hall of Fame. Many folks were put off by his tough-guy demeanor, but I liked him immediately. There was a kind of rough-cut charm about him and that what-me-worry way of navigating the world, and in that regard, he brought to mind another athletic Panamanian I would meet and fancy that year: the world lightweight champion Roberto Duran, a recovering street urchin from Panama City who appeared to me quite as cocksure and comfortable in a prize ring, his world of structured mayhem, as Vasquez did on the back of a half-ton horse—aglide in a crouch, his black boots on the dash, at 40 miles an hour.

"Why is everybody congratulating me?" Vasquez asked in mock disbelief. "It was the easiest stakes I ever won in my life. She's a big-striding filly. You don't know how fast you're going. She broke good and kept running. That's all. Nothing to it!"

So came Ruffian, the new starlet of American racing; any skepticism I may have harbored about her, any petty resentment I may have felt for her upstaging the protagonist of my unpublished scribblings, began to fade the instant that I saw her in that paddock. Pricci had embroidered not a stitch when he called to tell me about her that night in May, but I had seen so many phenoms come and go, so many colored flares that exploded in a hiss of smoke, that my inclination was to reserve all judgments until I could comfortably decide for myself. Like everybody else in this game, I wanted to watch her do it again, and that chance came four weeks later, on July 10, when she showed up for another 5½-furlong dash for two-year-old fillies, the Astoria Stakes at Aqueduct. She arrived at the paddock gate with a flourish and a bow, clearly on the muscle and wound like a spring, so visually and kinetically the center of her world that I made her appearance the lead of my breathless exertions in prose the next day: "Ruffian came to the paddock with her eyes rimmed in white, dancing, bouncing, sashaying to the left and right, a source of crackling energy in this most subdued of settings at Aqueduct."

Copernica had not returned for a second humbling, but another sensation had arisen in the wiry shape of a bay filly named Laughing Bridge, a daughter of the speedy stallion Hilarious; she had just won a maiden race at Aqueduct by eight lengths in fast time and looked like the only creature in the race who could get close enough to Ruffian to breathe on her. The only thing different was the black filly's passenger. Vasquez, that rascal, had just been suspended by the stewards for careless riding, and in his place Whiteley had put Vincent Bracciale, a nice little rider known for his ability to carry out, simultaneously, three tasks that often proved too much for one rider's brain—that is, stay out of trouble, follow instructions, and, when in doubt, hold on. Frank's instructions to Vincent were characteristically terse: "Don't get her hurt, don't hit her, and don't get her beat." As Whiteley saddled Ruffian in the paddock, there was Vasquez sitting astride the lead pony in the next stall; in a highly unusual gesture for a leading rider, he had volunteered to take her to the post. Even Whiteley, normally dour at moments like this, had to smile at the sight of Vasquez on that pony.

"He doesn't want to let her get too far away," Frank said.

I settled in a box seat behind Whiteley. Because Ruffian had been running and working so fast, I naturally glanced at the program to see who owned the Aqueduct track record for this distance. Well, I thought, fancy meeting you here. It was Raise a Native, one of the fastest two-year-olds ever observed in the known cosmos, a muscle-bound steed whose speed was nearly as legendary as that of The Tetrarch's. Raise a Native had stopped the Teletimer in 1:02³/₅ on July 17, 1963. The way she had lately been flying around Belmont Park, Ruffian was surely fast enough to threaten that mark, and I loved the symmetry of the challenge. The muscle-rippling Raise a Native, a Charles Atlas of the species, was the fastest horse ever sired by Native Dancer, the immortal Grey Ghost whose only loss in twenty-two starts came in the 1953 Kentucky Derby, when he was carried wide on the first turn and lost by a diminishing head to Dark Star. Since Ruffian's mother, Shenanigans, was a daughter of Native Dancer, that made Raise a Native her blood uncle, and I remember thinking what a good story it would make to watch his baby niece slash the electric timer beam at 1:02³⁄₅ and thus tie old Uncle Raise's mark.

As good as she was in her maiden outing and the Fashion, she was even more dazzling in the Astoria, breaking fast out of the gate and running as though she truly loved it all—the feel of the wrist slap and bongo of her feet, the sudden sound of those weird, two-legged creatures screaming at her as she ran past, the feel of the Rockaway wind in her face. She opened a length on Laughing Bridge around the far turn, with Vincent just sitting on her, and the crowds glanced at the Teletimer as she sped through the first quarter: :21⁴⁄₅! Fast enough to keep Mumtaz Mahal busy. Braulio Baeza, on Laughing Bridge, was nudging his filly to keep in touch, and she was trying her best, but hers was a pointless chase to nowhere and Baeza knew it. Ruffian opened three lengths on her at the turn for home. Bracciale sat motionless. All eyes turned again to the infield clock and I saw Whiteley, smoking a cigarette, lean forward and look at the Teletimer as she swept through the first half-mile. The light flashed :44²⁄₅! Frank saw it and glanced down. He looked back up. Ruffian was opening a six-length lead. Vince did not move. Only three fillies had shown up to meet her that day and they were disappearing as Ruffian came home, until all that was left was Raise a Native's ghost, and she had him crying uncle through five eighths of a mile in a sensational :56²⁄₅, which is about as fast as horses run in Queens, and then the wire loomed just ahead and the crowd seemed to fall into a hushed silence waiting for her to catch that chestnut ghost. She bounded under the wire in 1:02⅘, just missing the record by a fifth of a second, and the crowds breathed out in one stentorian chorus: "Ooohhhhhh!"

She won by nine widening lengths over Laughing Bridge, who finished twelve lengths in front of the third filly, Our Dancing Girl. Ruffian had literally spread-eagled the field. If Vince Bracciale had asked her for anything extra, the record would surely have been hers. The *Daily Racing Form*'s official chart of the Astoria noted that she had won "with speed to spare."

Whiteley rushed past me and behind him came Stuart Janney and then Ogden Phipps, the patriarch of the Phipps family. Ogden was the only son of the late Mrs. Henry Carnegie Phipps, the grand dame of the sport, who had owned Bold Ruler and had kept his sperm in the family bank with the other family jewels, so to speak, not letting any of those little buggers swim too far from home. While keeping Bold Ruler's trysts as close to private as she could, Mrs. Phipps did grant her children access to the stallion. So it was that Ogden sent one of his best broodmares, Broadway, to the court of his mother's stallion, and out of this mating came that dark-brown son with the convex nose, Reviewer. It was all in the family, really, for Stuart Janney had married Ogden Phipps' full sister, Barbara Phipps, and it was through that web of human DNA that Reviewer's blood was mixed with that of Shenanigan's. And it was through that twining of equine DNA that we had, on this day in July of 1974, that winged thing in black chiffon now floating towards us in the summer heat, crunching down the ramp from the racetrack to the winner's enclosure. There Frank Whiteley was drinking a cup of cold water drawn from the cooler by the jockey's scale. Ogden saw him and came over.

"You need the water more than she does," Mr. Phipps said. Frank merely nodded. Ogden Phipps had seen and bred many nimble-footed fillies in his life, the last a beautiful

Jacinto Vasquez atop Ruffian at the 1974 Fashion Stakes

daughter of Buckpasser, his champion racehorse and stallion, out of the mare Intriguing, a daughter of Swaps. Her name was Numbered Account. Just three years earlier, the big bay had won seven stakes races for Phipps—among them the Fashion, the Spinaway and the Gardenia—on her way to being voted America's champion two-year-old filly. Now here was the sixty-five-year-old breeder, his hands jingling the change in his pocket, looking like an art professor in the Louvre as Ruffian came and turned and stood four-square before us. Phipps looked her up and down, his eyes glancing from that penciled head to those dainty feet.

"What do you think?" I asked.

He paused a moment, shy as he was, to think on that. "I've never seen a filly like this," he said quietly. "I thought Numbered Account was good at this stage, but this one—she'll sure beat the colts."

Phipps was not alone in trying futilely to recall a filly like Ruffian. In fact, it was right there at Aqueduct, in the wake of the Astoria, that those with any sense of racing history began to search the leas and hollows of memory for a juvenile filly who may have been able to run with her. I had seen a bevy of fast two-year-old fillies in my life, beginning with Doubledogdare and Leallah at old Arlington and running right through to Tosmah and Numbered Account and the undefeated La Prevoyante, the Canadian flyer, but none of those ever did it like this, ever did it all so fast and with such consummate ease. Trainer Al Scotti came through the paddock and spotted Pat O'Brien, a New York Racing Association vice president, and near bowled the VP over. Scotti, the trainer of Laughing Bridge, grabbed O'Brien by the arm. "Hey, Pat, I think you ought to give us a trophy for running against her," he said.

I found Baeza in the jock's room later. "What do you think about Ruffian, Braulio?" I asked him.

Baeza grew a cockeyed grin. "I *don't*," he said. "I *don't* think about her. I just chase her. I could have cut through the centerfield and she still would have beaten me."

Only Whiteley, who had already logged forty-three long years in the game, seemed inclined to play it down, to dismiss the enthusiasm of the racing crowd. This was not feigned contrariness on his part. The tendency to soft-pedal any brilliant feat by one of his own horses was intrinsic to his nature as a "wizened old horseman," a part of his conservative persona, and so there he was, after the race, pooh-poohing Ruffian's surpassing performance at Aqueduct that day. "She's been catching easy fields," he said. "Heck, she hasn't beat anything yet."

The Maryland native did allow that she was a sweetheart to be around and train. "She's perfect," he said. "She's got manners and she's got sense ... Anyone can train her. The good ones are dangerous in anyone's hands. The good ones make the trainers and the jockeys look good."

One day later in the week, in the stable area at Belmont Park, Whiteley was pacing around his shed at the close of a morning at work as Ruffian, in her stall, was burying her nose in a tub full of oats. She heard his voice and raised her nose and came to the door of her stall. I was telling Frank of what Ogden Phipps had said about her being the best filly he had ever seen, a young gazelle without an equal in his long experience as an observer of the turf, and of how Phipps had said that she could beat the colts for sure if given half a chance. Ruffian stood at the door of the stall and looked at Whiteley as if to say, "Well?" Philosophically, Whiteley said, he was opposed to running fillies against colts, expressing a belief shared fervently by every old-school horseman in the world.

"I like to keep them where they belong," Frank said. Yet he knew what people like Phipps were saying about her. Looking at Ruffian, Frank added, "But, with her ... " He shrugged. "But if I *do* run her against colts, it *won't* be until the fall," he said. "I just keep my fingers crossed and hope she stays sound. In this business, one minute you have a horse, and the next minute you don't."

I had returned to the track to see Ruffian perform at a strange, unsettling time, and not just to a sport besieged and rimmed by seedy off-track betting parlors, by diminishing crowds, by a deepening state of ennui. The nation was in turmoil. The war was lost and even then you could see the whole bloody trail ending on the rooftop of the U.S. Embassy, with the VC crawling up the back stairwell, dusting for prints. In my rush to leave Saigon, I had left my recorder and tapes under my bed at the Prince Hotel on Tran Hung Dao, and it pleasured me now to imagine some VC colonel lying on his back on my mattress, staring at the ceiling fan and listening in curious wonder to the call of Damascus winning the Travers by twenty-two. Nixon was even more lost than the war—he was still fighting to keep his own tapes, none of them starring Damascus and Dr. Fager—but this was June of 1974 and he was just two months away from the door of that helicopter, and all his buddies were lost or gone or going to jail. It was June 19, a hot day on Long Island, and I was heading for Manhattan to see my book editor at Dutton, Laurie Colwin, and on the way I swung by Belmont Park to see jockey Robyn Smith about a story I wanted to write about her. This was years before she fled the track, ran off with widower Fred Astaire, got hitched to him and then, after Fred died, became a commercial pilot. She was quite beautiful and looked especially striking on the back of a fire-breathing thoroughbred. Robyn was also riding very well, to be sure, but trainers were hitting on her all the time and the pressure was beginning to wear her down. All she wanted to do was ride.

So I went to Belmont Park to see her ride in the first race of the day. I had seen many horses break down and die and had seen too many jockeys in too many spills, but what I saw that early afternoon was so disturbing as to haunt my dreams for months, and even today I sometimes think of it whenever I see petunias in long pots, or see grooms hosing down their horses' necks on boiling summer days, or see Allen Jerkens, one of the world's leading horsemen, walking upright down victory lane at Belmont Park. Robyn was riding Coup Landing, a nine-year-old gelding who used to be one of the fastest sprinters in New York, a winner of twenty-six races and almost $220,000 in purses, but lately had been slipping slowly down the claiming ranks and now he was nearing the bottom in New York. This was a race for $25,000 selling platers. Why, there was a time when Coup Landing would have had this bunch for lunch, with a quart of sweet feed on the side. I hung with the grooms on the fence along victory lane and then, above the din, I could hear Dave Johnson, the track announcer, calling Coup Landing's name as Robyn urged him forward on the far turn. "And here comes Coup Landing on the outside!" Old as he was, the bugger no longer had the lick he once had, but he was still as bulldoggedly tough as ever and he was passing horses one by one through the lane, until finally Robyn had him in the clear and she sent him home to win it all by two. She stopped him around the clubhouse turn and brought him back around to us, to a gathering of cheers. "Way to go, Robyn!" they yelled. She smiled and waved. She walked the horse down victory lane to the winner's circle and the bettors chattered like chipmunks over the acorn she had just tossed at their feet. Coup was paying off at the rate of $6.20 for a $2 bet. Robyn had her picture taken in the winner's circle, waved again, and then slid off the horse.

I met her as she was walking away down victory lane. Her cheeks were flecked with sand. "Nice ride," I said.

"He's a gem," she said. "A real old pro."

A voice cried out from behind her. "Robyn! Your horse has collapsed. Your horse is down!"

She spun around. Coup Landing lay sprawled on his left side, in the middle of the winner's circle, thrashing his feet in the air as he tried to regain his legs. The horse looked in a panic. The lapping crowds stood staring in circular disbelief. Smith started towards her fallen horse. Coup's groom, Bobby Jeans, held in his hands the reins of the bridle and urged the gelding to his feet. The horse flailed his legs wildly in the air. He panted and paused and panted again, looking tired and confused, like a broodmare in the middle of a breached birth. More people came to the scene, converging from the clubhouse and the grandstand, their faces pinched and grimacing in pain as the old warrior waved his arms in the heat. Hands covered faces. There were angry shouts.

"Help him!" someone yelled.

"Let's try to get him up," shouted Henry Meade, another of Coup's handlers, to Bobby Jeans. "Put some water on his head."

Robyn went to the watercooler. Jeans handed the reins to Meade and picked up the end of the garden hose in a corner of the circle. They all thought it was heat-stroke. I looked in the horse's eyes and they were glazed. Meade tugged on the reins, urging Coup Landing to get up. The horse raised his heavy shoulders and planted his front hooves on the cinders and, like some giant newborn foal, dug his forelegs into the ground and pushed, raising himself to his feet. The crowds erupted in cheers. Coup Landing wobbled forward, teetering, staggering as Meade led him in a circle. Robyn came forward with a handful of water from the cooler and tossed it on the horse.

Meade shouted at her. "Get back, Robyn. He could fall on you."

Coup's legs began to buckle again.

"I want to put water on him," she yelled to Meade. He waved at her and told her to stay back.

"Get a bucket of ice!" somebody yelled.

Coup wobbled and fell again, this time pitching forward, dropping like a stunned fighter to his knees, his white nose punching into the box of fuchsia-colored petunias by the jockeys' scale. He had rapped his teeth hard on the box and now Meade leaned back and hauled the reins and pulled him up and off the flowers. The horse grew more unsteady as he wobbled after Meade. And then he toppled over again, fell of a piece like a tree, but his eyes were open and he lay on his left side with his legs sweeping slowly over the stone base of the winner's circle as though he were running in a dream, not fast but running, and then he stiffened, his legs quivering, and the stable workers came and gathered round him as the crowds of bettors fell silent again. Coup's Hobeau Farm trainer, Allen Jerkens, was there, towering over him, looking helpless and sad. Two more Jerkens grooms, Peter Gay and Ralph Theroux, saw what was happening, and Gay said, "Let's go over there, maybe we can help." They jumped the clubhouse fence and sprinted toward the winner's circle and so now they were all there, Allen and Henry, Bobby and Gay, Ralph and Robyn, and then Dr. Manuel Gilman, the track's examining veterinarian, swam through the circle of friends and kneeled next to the horse. He thought it was sunstroke too.

"Run some cold water on this horse," Gilman said. So Peter Gay held the hose and ran the water on the horse's face and neck while Robyn Smith sat down by his head and patted his nose with a handful of ice and wiped the grains of sand out of his mouth. The sand on her cheeks was running off and she was leaning forward over the horse's head and wiping from his eyes the dirt he had picked up before he swung out from behind those horses on the turn.

"Come on, Coup," she said. "Come on, Coup. Get up. Come on … "

Gilman put his hands on the horse. "Get the oxygen somebody!" he yelled. Jeans and Meade jumped up and ran to the ambulance parked on the racetrack. I was crouching right next to Robyn. Now the horse grew very still. The circle fell quiet. I closed my notebook and looked up and around, and even today, I can still see them all standing and sitting there in that little circle of windless light at Belmont Park. It's like some old and frayed filmstrip I carry around in my head—Bobby and Henry coming with the oxygen and Allen wiping his eyes with the back of his hand and Robyn murmuring to the horse between sighs and then Doc Gilman saying:

"He's dead. Forget it, he's dead."

Allen Jerkens tipped back his head, his eyes raised and blinking fast, and Bobby Jeans stooped over and patted his horse a last time on the neck while Gay turned the water off and Ralph walked away and Robyn Smith slumped over—she never looked more beautiful—dropping her forehead on his neck, and said, "Oh, no. Come on, Coup. Come on."

Coup Landing had died of a burst aorta, was dying even as Meade led him in circles, and I talked to several old-timers that day, and they all said Coup was the only horse they had ever seen or heard of who died in any winner's circle. Later that afternoon I walked into the *Newsday* offices and went straight to my desk and was shuffling papers around when I saw Dick Sandler, the sports editor, coming towards me. I did not want to write the Coup Landing story. I knew it was a good story to tell but I thought I had gotten too close to it, kneeling next to Robyn and all, and didn't want to relive it. I was thinking I may not tell Sandler about it but I knew I had to say something.

"Were you at Belmont today?" he asked.

"Yeah, briefly. I had to go into the city."

"A story came over the wires about a horse that died in the winner's circle," he said. "You know anything about it?"

I fumbled with a sheaf of papers, feigning indifference. "Oh yeah, I saw that," I said.

Sandler's deputy, Sandy Padwe, heard this and drifted over.

"What did you see?" Sandy asked.

I was feeling trapped now, impatient. "A horse named Coup Landing died in the winner's circle. He won the race. Robyn had her picture taken with him. She hopped off and was walking away when he collapsed."

Sandler and Padwe looked at each other. They began to sound like homicide detectives.

"Where were you? In the press box?" Sandler asked.

"I was with Robyn."

"When he died?" Sandy asked.

"No, when he won the race. I was riding shotgun."

Sandler rolled his eyes. I pulled out my notebook and started reading from it. "I was walking with Robyn when the horse collapsed. She turned around and ran back to him. I went with her. He took a long time to die. He got up and fell into the flowerpots. He got up again. Then he collapsed again. Robyn sat down by his head. She rubbed ice cubes on his face. I crouched next to her. The crowds were yelling for us to help him. The stable workers were all there. Trainer was there. They talked to each other. They brought out a hose to run water on him because they thought he had heatstroke. Robyn was picking dirt out of his eyes. He died with Robyn sitting by his head and talking to him. Doc Gilman came over and said, 'He's dead … ' "

The two editors looked at each other again. "That's a hell of a story," Dick said.

"I'd really rather not … " I said. "You know, I used to groom and work with these animals and it's not easy watching one die like that."

"Why did you take all those notes if you didn't intend to write it?" Sandy asked.

"Because that's what I do. I watch things and take notes. I'm well-trained, like a seal."

Sandler waved me to the door of his office. "I don't get it," Dick said. "Why don't you want to write it?"

I was beginning to feel angry. "You wanna know why, Dick? Because I felt like a goddamn voyeur out there. The horse is down and Robyn's sitting there in tears and the trainer Allen Jerkens is in tears and the grooms are all weepy-eyed and the bettors are hanging over the fence, and they're all crying, and I'm standing in the middle of it with my notebook out and scribbling like some idiot stenographer, like a peepingfuck-ingtom with a press credential. And now you want me to write about it?"

Sandler started to walk away. He turned back. "That's nuts," he said. "A reporter's job is to report. When you worked for me on city side and you covered a fire or that car accident that killed all those kids in Huntington, did you stand around there worrying that you were a voyeur?"

"Those were news stories," I said.

"What is this?"

"Horses die all the time out there!" I said. "Morning and afternoon. It's the Charge of the Light Brigade. Boom! Another one bites the dust!"

"In the winner's circle? With the jockey sitting by his head? With all those hard-bitten horseplayers hanging on the fence?"

I had no place to go. "What the hell's wrong with me?" I finally said. "I was completely dry-eyed out there. I didn't even get choked up. It's like I had no feelings. I'm just there taking notes. Am I dead?"

We had moved into his office and he was settling in the chair in front of his desk. I had known Dick since I was a cub reporter in the Ronkonkoma office of *Newsday*, covering the Town of Islip. He was my mentor, my first editor, a Jew who had become my rabbi. He had been named as sports editor while I was on leave to write about Secretariat. He had taught me the craft on city side. How to chase a story down. How to stay on target. How to skirt the obstacles that folks are always planting in your way to prevent you from getting to a story, or from getting too close to the heart of one.

And now he was telling me how a reporter had to stay close to a story but somehow above it, on it yet detached from it, in it but somehow outside of it. "You can't afford to get emotionally involved," he said. "This job would eat you alive if you got too involved that way. You're not dead. You're protecting yourself. You've got to."

And so late that afternoon I sat down, in spite of myself, and wrote the Coup Landing story. The horse's death was no one's fault. He had a heart attack. But watching the old gelding die as that little human drama played out around him was as wrenching as anything I have witnessed, and through it, I began to sense a kind of subtle but decided shift in the way I viewed the sport—away from the old romantic notion, shaped by those summers at Arlington and all that reading I had done in college and toward a picture framed by cannon bones and inked in darker and more somber hues. Secretariat and Ruffian were throwbacks to those more innocent days. I knew them and where they came from, knew the stories in their separate histories, had traced them in a direct tail-male line back to the Darley Arabian, the refined, perfectly made Syrian stallion who was born in the desert outside the port of Aleppo in 1700, in a herd owned by a Bedouin warrior named Sheikh Mirza II, and imported to England by a British consul, Thomas Darley. Darley had offered the sheikh three hundred gold sovereigns for the horse and the sheikh had accepted it. Alas, he then reneged on the deal, thinking the horse too beautiful to lose. Thomas Darley wanted the colt very badly. So he arranged for a gang of renegade sailors to steal him and smuggle him out of Syria through Turkey. The Darley Arabian arrived in Yorkshire, by way of Smyrna, in 1704.

One of the great attractions of thoroughbred racing is that all the big names are connected. Not the Whitneys and the Vanderbilts, but the Bold Rulers and the Native Dancers. All those limbs on all those trees trace back in blood to a few thick roots buried in 250 years of unlost time. The only thing you need to know is that the Darley Arabian was twice bred to Betty Leedes (1705), daughter of the stallion Old Careless (1692) out of Cream Cheeks, and from the first union came Flying Childers—the fastest horse ever seen on planet Earth up to that time—and from the second came Bartletts Childers (1716). Bartletts Childers begat Squirt (1732), who begat Marske (1750), who begat the famed Eclipse (1764), undefeated runner extraordinaire, who begat Pot8os (1773), who begat Waxy (1790), who begat Whalebone (1807), who begat Sir Hercules (1826), who begat Birdcatcher (1833), who begat The Baron (1842), who begat Stockwell (1849), who begat Doncaster (1870), who begat the mighty Bend Or (1877), he of the gold coat and black spots, who begat Bona Vista (1889), who begat Cyllene (1895), who begat Polymelus (1902), who begat the lovely Phalaris (1913), who begat Pharos (1920), who begat the surpassing and undefeated Nearco (1935), who begat the unruly Nasrullah (1940), who begat the fleet Bold Ruler (1954), who begat Reviewer (1966), who begat Ruffian (1972), tall and strong, who at this very moment was grinding on the bit between her teeth and pulling groom Minnor Massey from the receiving barn around the clubhouse turn at Monmouth Park, on the New Jersey shore, while trainer Frank Whiteley was dousing another cigarette and popping another Gelusil and half running to keep up, a half a length in front of me and my panting shadow.

"Slow down!" Frank called to Massey. "I'll be winded before I get to the paddock."

It was July 27, late on a sunny afternoon, and Ruffian was heading to the Monmouth paddock to get saddled for the $104,480 Sorority Stakes, a three-quarter-mile dance for two-year-old fillies. The racing in New York in those days was so extraordinary—it was the epicenter of the sport in America—that I rarely found a need to leave town. I had never been to Monmouth, but I drove down there because Ruffian was heading for the clash of her young life, an encounter with the equally undefeated Hot n Nasty, a diminutive but brilliantly fast babe who had won her three starts by thirteen lengths, twelve lengths and 3¼ lengths. Those margins looked vaguely familiar. Hot n Nasty's last victory came in the Lassie Stakes at Hollywood Park, where she threw a buzz-sawing half mile in :44⅘ at Miss Tokyo, the darling of the California juvenile fillies, and cut her in half on the way to a scorching six furlongs in 1:09 flat. Ruffian had thrown down two fat-free workouts at Belmont since she'd won the Astoria, one a half-mile in :45 flat, and her racehorse body and running times were such that the bettors, barely scratching their heads, sent her off heavily favored at odds-on of 3-10, Hollywood Hot n Nasty notwithstanding.

It was a stupendous show from the break to the wire. Ruffian had never given up the lead once she had snatched it in a race, usually a few jumps away from the barrier, and she had never had another horse come look her in the eye once she got those quick-twitch gaskin, hindquarter and forearm muscles driving underneath her. Not one hundred yards out of the gate, it became clear that this would not be another easy-breezy day at the races. There were a couple of other manes and tails in the Sorority, but this was never anything but a two-horse duel. Vasquez was back on Ruffian, and he let her settle for the first seventy-five yards as jockey Darrell McHargue sent Hot n Nasty rushing to the lead. Twenty-five yards later, Ruffian was moving in long, powerful strides down the backside, and she caught Hot n Nasty and stuck her nose in front. Then a neck in front. Then a half a length as she bounded through the opening quarter in :21⅗, a blistering pace, with Hot n Nasty on the outside. McHargue told me later that he knew this was no stroll down the boardwalk.

"I knew we were tripping right along," he said. "We knew Ruffian had the speed, and the strategy was, if Ruffian took the lead, we'd lay right next to her." That was precisely what McHargue was doing now. The black had never hooked a filly who could run with her, not Copernica and not Laughing Bridge, but she had found one now and was hooked good as they made the turn and Vasquez asked her for more juice, but could not pull away. "I was surprised," Vasquez said after the race.

So were most of the other 26,133 people who came to see the duel. They were stirring in their seats as the fillies made the far turn and jumping to their feet at the peak of the arc as Hot n Nasty, at McHargue's urging, raced to within a neck of Ruffian, then a head. In a trice they were nose and nose, the big black and the little bay charging along at forty miles an hour like two young gazelles, mother and daughter, racing across a dusty African savanna. They pulled away from the other two and now they were all alone. And then, suddenly, it happened. McHargue made a clucking sound and Hot n Nasty thrust her nose in front. Yikes! This was something altogether new. Vasquez asked Ruffian for more and she picked up the beat and stuck her nose back in front. She was a head in front as they wheeled into the homestretch through a half-mile in a paint-peeling :44⅕. The trees swayed at Monmouth Park. Vasquez clucked to Ruffian. He chirped to her. He cajoled and coaxed and rubbed on her. The jockey sensed she might be hurting: she was trying to get out, drifting to the right, usually a sign that something is pinching a horse. Ruffian could not pull away from Hot n Nasty. So, as they neared midstretch, Vasquez reached back and smacked her with the whip. Gradually, irresistibly, stride by stretching stride, she pulled away. She was half a length in front with 220 yards to go. His whip in his right hand, Vasquez struck her on the flank again. She dug deeper, responding to Vasquez's urgent call, and finally pulled away as Hot n Nasty weakened in the final drive. Ruffian won it by 2¼ lengths in 1:09, a stakes record.

As fast as she got it done, I did not like her race and viewed the Sorority as something of a disappointment, however mild. She was not the airy-going filly I had seen blow through the Fashion and the Astoria. No one mentioned it then, but Vasquez would later say that she had popped a cold splint, a bony spur off a cannon bone, and that explained why she was trying to bear out; she was running from the pain that it was causing her. And Whiteley was later to confide that Ruffian woke up the next morning with a bad cough that hung around for days, nearly interrupting her championship campaign, and that he never really thought she was herself the afternoon of the Sorority. Frank was still digesting what he'd seen in the race when I finally caught up with him on the track. He was chasing after Minnor Massey and black beauty as they danced, cheek to cheek, back to the Monmouth Park shed. A patina of sweat made highlights on Ruffian's fur coat, darkening it even more than usual, and her sunlit muscles glistened like a seal's slipping from a bath of cold water.

"What did you think of her race?" I asked.

"She had to run good and hard today," Frank said.

I was jogging to keep up. "After her last race, at Aqueduct, you said, 'She hasn't beat anything yet.' Now what do you think?"

"She sure hooked something today," he said. "She's got some class to her."

His head down, having said all he wanted to say, Whiteley walked on. I yelled after him: "Where from here?"

"Saratoga, maybe … "

. . . . . . . . . . . . . . . . .

In 1930 and contrary to his mother's wishes, Frank Yewell Whiteley Jr. left his family's farm in Centreville, on Maryland's Eastern Shore, and began his career high-stepping after horses in barns and sheds all over the Free State. He was fifteen, and the Great Depression was just a year old, a circumstance that goes at least a furlong towards explaining why Frank spent a lifetime lamenting that the exigencies of survival had forced him to spend the first nickel he had ever earned. Like all young men who ever dreamed of being a horseman, Frank did all there was to do around horses, and he did it on the leaky-roof circuits of Delaware and Maryland in years when the specter of want rapped on the screen door and hung from the stable eaves. He walked hots. He groomed horses. He took out his first trainer's license at a little bullring called Marlboro, twenty miles east of the nation's capital, in 1936. He learned at tracks like Pimlico and Laurel, his home base. He learned how to mix country medicines for cheap, sore-legged horses and he learned from old-timers the most time-honored of balms: the cold-water hosing of horses' legs to reduce swelling and numb pain. Like the finest artisans in his craft, he never took a vacation, not once in his life, and worked long, brutal hours, finding God in the minutest details of his art. He was often seen outside his shed in midmorning, sitting on a chair and running a hose on a horse's legs; and if an inquiring reporter persisted in interrupting him at his work, Whiteley was not above ventriloquizing his impatience through the hiss of the hose turned full blast on the inquirer, as he once did to a former Miss America turned sports broadcaster. Like trainer Tom "Silent Tom" Smith, Seabiscuit's conditioner, Whiteley could be terse, ornery and plain hostile in his dealings with the media, and he owned no tolerance for the occasional stupid question. At a press conference at Churchill Downs in 1967, when he had Damascus entered in the Kentucky Derby, someone asked him one for the ages: "Mr. Whiteley, what are Damascus's sleeping habits?"

"How the hell would I know?" Whiteley shot back. "I ain't never slept with him!" Throwing his arms in the air, he got up and bolted from the room. This truculence made Whiteley an easy target in the papers, and he led with his chin most famously when the *Daily Racing Form*'s Charles Hatton, at the time the aging dean of American turfwriters, wanted to know whether Whiteley might run Damascus in the Woodward Stakes after the horse's twenty-two-length romp in the '67 Travers. Rarely did columnists in the *Racing Form* write a discouraging word about establishment trainers, so the acidic sarcasm of the Hatton column had the racetrack buzzing after it hit the stands. Whiteley was more than his usual crusty self, and the interview did not go well:

By Charles Hatton

AQUEDUCT, N.Y., Sept. 5—It is scarcely news any more when Damascus wins a race. He has got into a bit of a rut and won four straight. But there was big news behind the news when trainer Frank Whiteley went so far as to indicate what he proposes to do next with Mrs. Edith Bancroft's valuable property. In the press box, straws were drawn to see who would put this piquant question. Like a condemned man, the one with the short straw took a long breath, shook hands all around and was wished rotza ruck.

Came the confrontation: "What about the Woodward?" the delegate quavered.

"Humph!" the great trainer replied, in the original Potawotami.

Seeing that he was warmed up, full of information and chatty small talk, the interviewer pressed the point.

"That's the plan," the trainer rattled on, practically filibustering. "Now I gotta git these horses out!"

End of interview. The whole penance took 30 seconds.

Not a few veteran horsemen came of age viewing writers of the racing scene as beer-swilling, ink-stained nuisances who did not really work for a living and hence treated them as they so often treated their own bill-paying owners, with the sensitivity of the average mushroom farmer: *Keep them in the dark and throw a little shit on them every once in awhile. They* do *need to eat!* The racetrack is an insular world inhabited by horsemen who devote enormous amounts of energy to keeping from each other useful, even vital, information about their horses—from their animals' health and state of well-being and fitness to their specific plans and goals for their charges. In searingly competitive places and times, these are guarded like state secrets on shed row. Whiteley came of age on a bullring circuit where his very survival depended on revealing as little as possible about his horses, where he knew the object of the game was to outthink and outfox his ablest opponents in the game of claiming the best horses and winning the most races, and he got so good at playing it that his admiring rivals began calling him the Fox of Laurel. Naturally reticent, instinctively suspicious of the prying press, he held his hand so close to the vest that he also wore with pride another moniker: the Maryland Sphinx. No wonder, then, that he drove so many writers crazy with his bluster: They wanted precisely what he was, by training and instinct, most reluctant to give up.

Whiteley knocked around the Maryland tracks with cheap horses until his late forties, when he began to win bigger races with better animals for clients whose pedigrees matched those of their finest charges. His first highborn owner of serious means was Raymond Guest, the U.S. ambassador to Ireland from 1965 to 1968, for whom Whiteley trained champion Tom Rolfe, winner of the 1965 Preakness, and a flying son of Bold Ruler named Chieftain. His clients stepped into his shed right out of the Social Register. Mrs. Edith Woodward Bancroft, the daughter of former Hanover Bank president William Woodward, who chaired the Jockey Club for twenty years, gave him to train Damascus, the most capable male horse he ever laid his hands on, and Stuart and Barbara Janney gave him Icecapade ... and then Ruffian.

Training for the Janneys was like training for British royalty. Stuart was the very essence of the English country gentleman, American style. Born to the manor, he was with manners born. His father, Stuart Sr., was a prominent Maryland attorney, and his uncle, horseman Jervis Spencer, was a five-time winner of the Maryland Hunt Cup, one of the most grueling races in the world. He steeplechased after his uncle into the rolling Maryland countryside, and he saw his first flat race as a young boy. One day, at age thirteen, young Stuart was excused from classes at Gilman School in Baltimore to watch Man o' War win the 1920 Preakness Stakes at Pimlico. He began riding in hunt races at age sixteen and won four Maryland Hunt Cups in a riding career that spanned nearly three decades. He was Phi Beta Kappa at Princeton, a graduate of Harvard Law School, and a member of the 4th Marine Division during World War II, in which he was wounded while fighting in the Pacific. He wore country tweeds as comfortably as that leathery, wind-seamed grin. He had married Barbara Phipps in 1936, and when he and his wife decided to breed thoroughbreds at their Locust Hill Farm, outside Baltimore, Barbara's mother, Mrs. Henry Carnegie Phipps, encouraged them by handing over Rosie O'Grady's granddaughter Bold Irish. Of course it was out of Bold Irish, to Native Dancer's cover, that they got Shenanigans.

Saratoga is the greatest racetrack in America, the place where history breathes through every cornice and spire, where the very sun mounts up in livery and rides on horses slipping from their darkened stalls on ancient unraked spoors and heading in sets for the track. You can close your eyes and hear the roosters singing each to each and hear the sound of hoofbeats thumping past and the rhythmic breathing of the animals in their timeless circuits of the place. This was the town whose history always spoke of parasols and derby hats and tasseled surreys with the fringe on top, of eggs and bacon frying along the rows of sheds and of horses whinnying in the night. It was where the whole town stopped at the whistle blast of the trains that wheezed and snorted into the railroad station nearly every summer going back to the Civil War and where, minutes later, up the dusty main street past the United States and Grand Union hotels, the army of Negro grooms came leading strings of horses to the track across town, their heels clicking as they turned up Union Avenue, horses long dead now but whose names are embedded like dragonflies in the amber of their times. There was the mighty Man o' War and Exterminator, known as Old Bones, and there came Triple Crown winners Sir Barton and Gallant Fox and War Admiral, and later by train or van came the filly Top Flight and the weight-carrying Discovery, known as the Iron Horse, and came then the fleet Twenty Grand and C.V. Whitney's Equipoise, known as the Chocolate Soldier, and came unsung Seabiscuit and stretch-running Whirlaway, of whom Red Smith once wrote, "When Whirly turned on the heat, you could hear a frying sound." And home came Johnstown and Native Dancer, Nashua and Kelso, Damascus and Secretariat. They all came to The Spa to entertain the Carolina planters and the New York financiers for whom this had always been a retreat and playpen, a place for afternoon tea and scones.

This was the town where Subway Sam Rosoff, who built much of the New York underground, used to bring a half-dozen beautiful showgirls from Gotham to his home across the street from the entrance of the track and come five o'clock, as crowds poured out after the last race, there was Sam on his front porch, a cocktail in his hand and a lovely on each arm, waving to America's guests. This was where the illegal casinos thrived and Sophie Tucker came to sing and Harry Richman, in top hat and tails, sang "Puttin' on the Ritz." It was where Jack Benny used to sit on a rocker on the front porch of the Grand Union Hotel and Bing Crosby took evening walks with Don Ameche and Al Jolson plunged at the betting windows. This was where Mary Elizabeth Altemus Whitney, described by Alfred Vanderbilt as "America's most beautiful woman," used to come to the racetrack at 6 a.m. to see her horses work, still dressed in the evening gown she had worn the night before and now leading a kennel of her miniature dogs on a dozen sequined leashes. This was where Diamond Jim Brady, with precious stones encrusted on his underwear, escorted actress and singer Lillian Russell to the races and the betting parlors and where the rotund baron of barbed wire, John "Bet-a-Million" Gates, once lost $400,000 in a single day, only to return to win such a fortune from the teary-eyed handbooks that he needed a grocery basket to spirit the cash away. And this was where Man o' War got beat by Upset in the Sanford Stakes, 1919, and where Secretariat got beat by Onion in the Whitney Stakes and where, in one of the most dramatic races ever run on this continent, Ridan and Jaipur raced head and head for the full 1¼ miles of the 1962 Travers Stakes, with Jaipur finally winning it by the flare of his wet nostrils.

I always perceived myself as a late-19th-century man, not as Sister Carrie's lover wandering lost in the Brooklyn snow, but rather wandering lost in a dream, as a horseman, leaning under one of those giant elms in the Saratoga paddock while a colt as fine as Man o' War or Nashua or Secretariat comes walking towards me, the crowds parting amid a whir of voices and laughter in the air, men in tan suits and women in white polka-dot dresses gathering in a circle around the elm … Saratoga is for me the most idyllic, romantic place in the racing world, a Brigadoon that comes vibrantly alive one month of the year under peppermint awnings and oyster-shell skies. It was my annual journey into the irrecoverable past, my own mural-size daguerreotype, taken circa 1900. And so, in consequence, I saw it as perfectly fitting and proper that Ruffian should appear there one day in August of 1974 and summon from the sport's collective memory the undiminished legend of Mumtaz Mahal. For that is what

Ruffian did, to be sure, and it remains among the most cherished ways that I see and remember her now.

Ask Red Smith for the directions to Saratoga and here's what he would say: "The way to Saratoga is easy. From New York City, you drive north on the Thruway for 150 miles, take a left at Exit 14 onto Union Avenue, and go back about 100 years."

This is precisely how I got there in August of 1974 and ended up at the Turf Bar, having the usual blue plate special—roasted chicken, mashed potatoes and corn on the cob—with my good friend Andrew Beyer. All you need to know about Andrew now is how he spent his four years at Harvard, a tale he tells briefly in his excellent book *Picking Winners*, a tome credited with educating thousands of young horseplayers in how to bet using what Beyer calls his "Speed Figures":

"When I went to college my resolution to become a diligent scholar was undermined by the discovery that four racetracks lay within easy commuting distance of Harvard Square. I managed to dabble at both academic and equine pursuits for the better part of four years, until an irreconcilable conflict arose two weeks before graduation. My final examination in Chaucer was scheduled on the same day that Kauai King would be trying to win the Triple Crown at Belmont Park. I knew nothing about *The Canterbury Tales* but I did know something about Amberoid in the Belmont Stakes. So I went to the track. Although I blew a $12,000 education, I did collect a $13 payoff on Amberoid, cutting my losses for the day to $11,987."

Andy was then the turfwriter for the *Washington Star-News* and already on his way to becoming the father of the popular Beyer Speed Figures. Using this handicapping methodology, he was able to calculate the quality of a horse's performance in any given race by first determining the speed of the racing surface over which the horse performed. Since the speed of racing surfaces differs widely from track to track—and even from day to day at the same track—a horse's final running time is meaningful only

Mary Elizabeth Altemus Whitney at Saratoga

if the speed of the surface is known. A wiz at crunching numbers, Beyer had invented a way to do that mathematically and come up with a number, or fig, which would quantify just how fast a horse ran on a particular day. So while Ruffian's clocking of 1:02⅘ simply meant to the casual observer that she was a fifth of a second off Raise a Native's track record, it meant far more to Beyer. He had determined, by crunching numbers involving final times turned in by other horses who had won on the day of the Astoria, that the Aqueduct racing surface on that afternoon was not all that fast. Most two-year-olds do not run a fig of more than 100. Secretariat had run figs as a two-year-old that were in the low 120s, truly astronomical for a horse of that age, and in the 130s as a three-year-old, with his best being a 139 in the Belmont Stakes. Beyer had thought he might never again see a two-year-old run figures near those of Secretariat. And then, he told me in the Turf Bar that night, along came Ruffian.

"Her race in the Astoria was in the Secretariat range," Andy said. "As good as people think she is, I suspect she may be even better. She is truly phenomenal."

The Spinaway Stakes, Ruffian's next target, was just a few days away, and what seemed clear was that she was her old self again. Whiteley actually thought she might have to pass the Spinaway, the way the cough persisted, but she got over it just in time. He kept her training at Belmont Park, rather than at The Spa, and she had the downstate clockers raving over two of her moves on the training track: a half-mile in :47 flat on August 9 and five-eighths of a mile in :59⅕ four days later. I blinked when I first saw those numbers, thinking they were way too high, but I called a clocker down below and found out that grounds crews had been working on the training track and that the surface was deep and slow. In fact, Ruffian was moving as if on wings. Laughing Bridge had come back faster and better than ever after Ruffian had crushed her in the Astoria. She had already won two stakes races in a row at Saratoga, including a massive thirteen-length score in a division of the Schuylerville Stakes and a five-length romp in the

Adirondack Stakes. Stuart Janney was openly expressing worries that Laughing Bridge might be dangerously hard to handle. "She scares me a little," he said. She did not scare Beyer. He calculated the fig for Laughing Bridge's two Spa scores and waved her away. Outside of the Pope, no one spoke ex cathedra more eloquently than Beyer. His expressions of absolute certitude were part of his charm, and here he had crunched the numbers and was uttering his opinion without a twinge of doubt.

"Laughing Bridge doesn't have a chance against Ruffian," he said at the Turf Bar. "It's not even close. Al Scotti is kidding himself if he thinks he can beat her. Laughing Bridge is very fast, but she is not in Ruffian's league. She would be better off running against the colts in the Hopeful. She actually has a chance to win that." The Hopeful Stakes, the big two-year-old race at Saratoga, usually contested by young males, was being run the day after the Spinaway. So Beyer and I came up with a plan.

To save Al Scotti from himself and allow Andy to make a little bet on Laughing Bridge in the Hopeful, we decided to sit Al down and tell him that he must avoid Ruffian in the Spinaway and enter Laughing Bridge against those colts. Indeed, the next day we found Al in front of the racing secretary's office and asked him to join us on a little park bench that faced the lemonade stand outside the jock's room. Scotti looked at us curiously, wondering what this was all about.

"Bill and I have been thinking," Andy said, "and we have concluded that you shouldn't run Laughing Bridge in the Spinaway. You should run her instead in the Hopeful. She has run two big races up here and my speed figures suggest that she is running fast enough to beat the colts. Plus, the Hopeful may end up in two divisions because there's no standout."

Scotti looked at Andy, then at me, then raised his palms up. "I don't get it," Al said. "She's run two big races up here and you're tellin' me she's got no chance in the Spinaway?"

Andy and I went at him in relays. "That's exactly what we're tellin you, Al," I said. "We think it's a mistake. You're much better off in the Hopeful."

"Against all those colts?" Scotti said. "I don't know." Scotti shook his head.

Andy leaned forward, his arms gesturing and his voice deep and measured: "Laughing Bridge has no chance against Ruffian. None. Forget that Ruffian is a filly. She is better than all the colts. And Laughing Bridge has been running fast enough to beat the colts. We just think you should put her where she has the best chance."

Scotti was beginning to look edgy, uncomfortable. He rose from his seat. "I want to talk to Kenny Noe about this," he said. "I'll be right back." Noe was the racing secretary, the horsemen's head man. Scotti disappeared into Noe's office. Five minutes later, he reappeared, looking cheerily relieved. He walked towards us shaking his head.

"Kenny told me to stay where I am," Al said. "He doesn't believe in running two-year-old fillies against colts. I'm running in the Spinaway."

I reached out and shook Al's hand. "Good luck," I said. "I think you'll need it."

Ruffian had arrived in Saratoga on Tuesday, three days before her race, and on Thursday morning Whiteley sent her out for a final tightener. She was a picture of grace and power in motion. She smoked through three furlongs in a fiery :33⅘, *breezing*, and the next day came to the paddock for the Spinaway bouncing like a stud horse to the breeding shed, looking as big and powerful as any colt, all one thousand pounds of her, bigger and tougher and stronger. Ruffian was back, but she would be without Vasquez, who was sitting out another suspension. Whiteley once again tapped Bracciale to replace him. The track was listed as fast, but rain had fallen that morning, leaving the surface stickier than usual and not as glib as it had been the day before, when a comely fireball named Desert Vixen, the three-year-old filly champion of 1973, had won a talent-rich race in 1:09⅘ for six furlongs, the same distance as the Spinaway. So there was something against which to measure Ruffian's performance.

She vaulted from the gate and went to the lead at once, breaking faster than she ever had, and leveled off down the backstretch in long, smooth strokes. She had a two-length lead at the end of a quarter-mile, relaxing as she never had before. Whiteley edged forward in his seat. She banked around the far turn all full of herself, waiting for the patient Bracciale to say the word, and then Bracciale glanced back and saw the face of Laughing Bridge and then Baeza asking Scotti's filly for more speed. Bracciale eased his hands forward just a notch. Ruffian felt the message and took off. "I could feel her spurt out from under me," he would say.

She raced to the head of the stretch three lengths in front, through a faster and faster half-mile, and left Scotti's filly spinning like loose paper in her gusting wake. Ruffian opened seven lengths at the eighth pole, 220 yards from the wire, and she continued drawing off as Bracciale eased her through the last one hundred yards. All kept turning from her to the blinking Teletimer and back to her. She finished in a gallop, 12¾ lengths in front of Laughing Bridge, and froze the Teletimer at 1:08⅗, the fastest six furlongs ever run by a two-year-old at this hoary old graybeard of a racing palace and only three-fifths of a second behind Spanish Riddle's track record. Had Vincent Bracciale merely asked her, no doubt she'd have eclipsed The Riddle's mark.

It was an extraordinary moment.

I was still listening to the roars of that jubilant crowd as I made my dash from the box seats down to the racetrack, where a shaken Al Scotti was standing near the scales and scuffing at the dirt, taking deep breaths and fluttering his lips when asked his thoughts on Ruffian's Spinaway. "How are you going to beat her?" Scotti said. "How? How can you get even close enough to beat her?" If he had any regrets about throwing Laughing Bridge to the lioness, he was not saying, but he had clearly learned his lesson. Whiteley had just arrived on the track and Scotti swept over to him, gesturing like a baseball umpire calling a runner safe. "No more, Frank," Al said, waving his arms. "No more."

Bracciale brought Ruffian to a halt before us, waved his crop at the stewards in their stand above the track—a signal meaning that all was well—and hopped off.

"How was the ride?" I breathed.

"Whew!" Bracciale said.

Stuart Janney now appeared in the winner's circle, beaming as he stood admiring his finest creation, from fetlock to forelock. "My, she did it easy," Janney said. He had heard Bracciale's exclamation and laughed. "You didn't have anything to worry about this time," Janney said.

"No, sir!" said Bracciale. "When I stood up under her at the wire, I could feel her accelerate under me. She was just galloping the last part of it. I don't know what to say. I really don't."

More than the swiftness of the victory, it was the ease and effortlessness of the performance that stunned even the most blasé of sophisticates, and what Ruffian did that hazy afternoon was only just beginning to dawn on the assorted waifs, brigands, gamblers and breeders who were standing now as one and giving her an ovation as the outrider led her towards that charmed circle down below. Alfred Vanderbilt, the man who had bred and raced Native Dancer, descended to the racetrack for a closer peek. "She looks like a three-year-old running against two-year-olds," said Vanderbilt, who had been attending races since the late teens of the century and had put together the Seabiscuit-War Admiral match race at Pimlico in 1938. "And she goes to the post unaccompanied by a pony. She has such sense and such manners."

For Baeza, chasing Ruffian had become his worst monotony. He was heading back to the jock's room, to wash the racetrack off his face, when I caught him from behind. "It's like chasing a ghost," he said. "I tell you one thing, she's got a good-looking behind. I know. I *ought* to know. I keep looking at it out there ... I tried to run with her around the turn but she just played with me. I moved up a couple of lengths, Ruffian looked at me and *pfftt!!* Goodbye."

Lucien Laurin, Secretariat's old conditioner, was as unabashedly frank as he was when he first saw the young filly in the paddock at Belmont Park: "As God is my judge, she's better than Secretariat was when he was a two-year-old."

Veteran rider Mike Hole had finished third on Scottish Melody, almost two lengths behind a staggering Laughing Bridge, and he had seen many fast horses come and go over the years but he had never witnessed one like this. "The main thing is that she holds together," he said.

"Why do you say that?" I asked.

Hole shrugged. "With all that speed, there's a lot of pressure on her legs. But if she holds together, she'll be a world-beater."

No surprise, of course, but I ended up chasing Whiteley chasing Ruffian back to the barn. He was shy and very old school and never lingered to hear the accolades. "This looked like her best race yet," he said. "She relaxed the first part of it. That's what *I* liked." He had been telling people that her extraordinary speed was a worry to him, and he clearly was uncomfortable with all the glib chatter he had been hearing about Ruffian's invincibility. Feeling exposed, he cocooned himself in her mortality. "She's gonna get beat," he said, trying to keep up with Minnor and the filly as they headed to the spit box for routine blood and urine tests. "They have to get beat someday. She's got speed and class, too, but I can't have her right every day. If you run 'em enough, they all get beat."

Ruffian's performance in the Spinaway was the greatest demonstration of unalloyed speed that I had ever seen in a two-year-old racehorse—male or female, recent or long past—and that she had done the fete at Saratoga, the ancestral home of American racing, only further consecrated it as historic. Beyer was saying that Ruffian was at least as good as, if not better than, Secretariat. "Secretariat, as a two-year-old, never ran a fig as big as Ruffian's in the Spinaway," he said. My own passing doubts about Ruffian had nothing whatever to do with her or anything that I had seen her do. I had been around racehorses and racetracks for twenty years, and I had never seen a two-year-old do what she was doing—and with an insouciance that bordered on the downright cavalier, moving as she pleased with a restrained grace and power and at velocities rarely seen in animals so young. She was, in my experience, sui generis. Whatever doubts I had traced not only to a natural skepticism aroused when I am confronted by anything that might be described as miraculous or magical, but also to my absolute refusal to believe that a Ruffian could materialize in the barely receding shadows of so dominant a figure as Secretariat. My own adventures as a turfwriter had become so impossible to fathom, so straight out of a storybook, that I was having trouble wrapping my brain around it. Try to imagine. Thirty months earlier I was writing about groundwater poisoning by cesspools in Quogue and ammonia stripping in the tertiary treatment plant in Lake Tahoe, Nevada, and since then I had witnessed the rise of the most surpassing racehorse the world had ever seen, a Greek discus thrower among the equines, and in his immediate wake I had beheld the spectacular entrance, stage right, of this most glorious of all fillies. How do you figure?

All Ruffian had to do now, to put an exclamation mark on her baby tour de force, was step out of her division and do to the colts what she had done to the fillies. No one doubted her ability to do that. It was a given. The proof was in the doing, though, and by the end of the Saratoga meet, it had become lustrously clear that the one colt she had to beat—the most talented male two-year-old colt in America—was a tough, athletic, muscle-bound little dude who was just as undefeated as she. His name was Foolish Pleasure. The day after the Spinaway, in the second division of the Hopeful, he came charging off a torrid early pace—faster even than the pace that Ruffian had set—

ran down the leaders just past midstretch and galloped on to win by almost four lengths. He did not run anywhere near her number, but he had stamped himself as a colt of considerable quality. Like Ruffian's Spinaway, the Hopeful was Foolish Pleasure's fifth straight victory, the last of four consecutive stakes wins, and it set off a clamorous tub-thumping which called for Ruffian to stop beating up on all those poor little girls and bloody the nose of somebody her own size. Frank knew all along, from the moment she started beating her sisters pointless, that he was going to have to ask her to dance with the colts. The most coveted title in racing is that of Horse of the Year, and Ruffian was very much a contender for that crown *if* she beat the boys in the greatest of New York two-year-old races: the one-mile Champagne Stakes at Belmont Park on October 5. Trainer LeRoy Jolley was aiming Foolish Pleasure for the Champagne.

The prospect of the two horses meeting was almost too delicious to contemplate. It was the talk of the racetrack that early autumn, an event that would surely be viewed as the race of the year. At least a half-dozen other colts would show up at the post, trying to pick up a scrap of the $145,000 purse, and the only question twisting in the wind off the Long Island Sound was how Foolish Pleasure would respond when Ruffian, doing what came naturally and what she did best, shot out of the gate and opened an early lead down the long Belmont backstretch. Vasquez was the regular rider of both the filly and the colt, but no doubt he would choose to pilot Ruffian—he was riding all of Whiteley's best horses—and just as surely Jolley would tap Braulio Baeza to ride Foolish Pleasure. He was the jock who steered him to victory in the Hopeful. So what would Jolley tell Baeza to do? Would he deny Ruffian a chance to relax on the lead? Would he force a withering early pace, one that would weaken them both, and set up a laggard to come from behind? Or would Baeza, more sensibly, lie just off Ruffian's early exertions and make one hard, determined run at her on the turn for home? These and other questions were dangling from the Belmont eaves when suddenly—tragically, it would turn out—the prospect of their meeting vanished in the shake of a thermometer. Whiteley was aiming his horse for the Champagne by way of the Frizette Stakes, another lucrative but pointless race against fillies, and Ruffian was her usual brilliant self on the eve of it. In fact, she had the clockers doing handsprings around Belmont Park when they caught her in a blistering three-eighths of a mile in :33²/₅. Next morning, Whiteley noticed that she hadn't finished her breakfast, the red flag that all horses fly when something is amiss. He took her temperature. She was running a slight fever. He called Janney and told him that Ruffian would not be running in the race. A day later, the trainer noticed something far more disturbing. He saw Ruffian take a couple of bad steps. So he told Massey to walk her up and down the shed while he studied her gait.

"You couldn't tell anything was wrong with her," Frank said. Taking no chances, he summoned her regular veterinarian, Dr. James Prendergast, to take X-rays. He found the problem: Ruffian was suffering from a hairline fracture of her right hind phalanx bone, an injury she probably incurred during her last wind-sail around Belmont Park. For all serious students of the thoroughbred breed, the broken bone was darkly ominous, as though a party of her ancestors were calling long distance. Reviewer had suffered his first cannon-bone fracture while finishing second in the 1968 Hopeful, his second at age three in the Wood Memorial, and a third at age four after running a close second in the Metropolitan Mile. At the age of eleven, Reviewer broke a hind leg in a paddock accident and had to be destroyed two weeks later when, following a change of casts, he went utterly berserk, lunging and leaping all over the place, and threatened to hurt himself or his handlers.

Shenanigan's sire, Native Dancer, had a career abbreviated by those mushy ankles, and he passed his unsoundness on to generations of talented horses by figuring prominently in two extraordinarily prepotent and popular sire lines—through his unsound son Raise a Native, the sire of the unsound but extremely prolific stallion Mr. Prospector, and through his daughter Natalma, the dam of the great stallion Northern Dancer, whose coveted blood has produced many brilliantly fast and fragile racehorses who in turn have bequeathed their strengths and weaknesses to whole tribes of runners around the world. So through the blood of Reviewer and Native Dancer—a double dose, top and bottom—Ruffian was blessed with unearthly speed yet cursed by this inherent fragility.

No one was learning the vicissitudes of racing any faster than I was in that autumn of my thirty-third year. In all the seasons I had spent at Arlington and Washington parks as a young horseplayer and a groom, watching nine races a day on endless cards, I had never once witnessed a horse break down or die of a heart attack or have to be put down. Never once did I see those long-faced attendants trundling to the track with The Screen. From nowhere in my rich, overstocked memory of those days could I conjure a single incident involving the demise of a racehorse. Not one that I had witnessed in the flesh. I had watched in a kind of detached horror, on television, as a stoutly bred colt named Black Hills, owned by Robert Kleberg of the King Ranch, broke his leg and went down at the moment when he was making a winning move on the turn for home in the 1959 Belmont Stakes, pitching jockey Eddie Arcaro face-down in the mud. Unconscious, Arcaro likely would have drowned had a Pinkerton guard not vaulted the outside fence, rushed to his side, and lifted his gurgling mouth out of the water. Black Hills had to be destroyed.

Horses have been breaking down since the days of Judas Ben-Hur, but in no way did that explain what I was seeing now. Something dark and ominous had moved like a shadow over the game between my last years at Arlington in the mid-1960s and the day in '72 when I walked into Belmont as a turfwriter. Horses were breaking down with a heightened, even gruesome, regularity. Some weeks, by my count, two or three or four would snap a bone and have to be put down by lethal injection. Precisely why these breakdowns were occurring at so alarming a rate became the subject of an intense, often heated, debate—one that would draw me in through a controversial story I wrote for *Sports Illustrated* and make me the target of wrath for literally scores of industry apologists. Veterinarians seemed to me suspiciously coy on the subject, but one California vet of considerable prominence told me that the increase in breakdowns could be traced directly to the growing use among backstretch vets of a powerful anti-inflammatory drug called cortisone. Cortisone reduced the painful swelling in horses' ankles and knees, allowing them to gallop and race sound for short periods of time, but it did nothing to heal the problems that caused such inflammation. In fact, feeling no pain, hard-trying horses only taxed their damaged joints even more and often broke down completely under the pressures of training and racing.

Cortisone aside, racehorses were simply not as sturdy as they were in the first sixty-five years of the century. The thoroughbred had grown finer and more fragile with each passing decade. Moreover, this inherent breakability had lately become more widespread because the most popular and coveted sire lines—the lines that produced the fastest horses in the world, the animals of extreme speed, and this in a sport truly drunk on speed—also carried with them the seeds of their own destruction: designer genes bearing markers of unsoundness. These were the termites in the walls of the breed. Ruffian was not without her own nest of them.

Just three hours before the running of the Champagne Stakes, I left the track and made my way to Whiteley's barn deep in the Belmont stable area. I had decided long ago that I would never visit his barn before ten o'clock in the morning, before the day's chores were largely done, and would never go for an interview without a specific purpose. I did not know this for sure, but I sensed he had no appetite for small talk.

Right or wrong, I had never had a moment's trouble with him, never heard a cross or angry word, and on this day he looked far more relaxed than ever, at ease with what had befallen Ruffian. He saw me coming and sat down in a chair by Ruffian's stall, his hat tipped jauntily back on his head, a smile on his face.

"What do *you* want?" he said. He was teasing.

"I want to write something about Ruffian for *Newsday* and *The Thoroughbred Record*," I said. "How's she doing?"

"See for yourself," he said.

Frank shifted in his chair and peered into the stall. Ruffian was dressed in four protective bandages and she was facing the rear of her classically unfurnished room. The moment she heard his voice, she craned her neck and faced the door, flashing that snip of white between her eyes. Seeing Whiteley outside, she now turned slowly in her stall and took a step or two until she appeared at the door. She dropped her head over the webbing, stopping foursquare. Pricking her feminine ears, she stared at the man who had brought her this far and listened to him as he spoke.

"Well, there she is," he said. "You can see there's nothing bothering her. If it were another horse, I might not have stopped her. But with her, I'm not taking any chances."

I told Whiteley that I knew how he felt about running fillies against colts and asked him if he had been really serious about his announced plans to run her in the Champagne. "Definitely," said Frank. "I was definitely thinking of doing that."

I stretched out my left hand, palm down, toward Ruffian's nose.

"Watch yourself," cautioned Whiteley.

She straightened her ears and sniffed the back of my hand. I felt the warmth of her breath and drew my hand away.

She was a month from being vanned with the outfit to Whiteley's winter quarters in Camden, South Carolina, and I was wondering what he had in mind for her in

1975. I knew that he had suffered two wretched experiences in the circuslike atmosphere of the Kentucky Derby; Tom Rolfe in '65 and Damascus in '67 had finished third, even though they both later proved to be the most talented horses in the race. The trainer was not shy in expressing his feelings of disdain for America's most famous test, but I had to ask him: "Is the Kentucky Derby a possibility?"

"She'll be nominated to the Kentucky Derby, yes," he said. "She'll be nominated for all the Triple Crown races. I plan to turn her out next month. She won't go back into any kind of training until those X-rays are perfectly clear. We have a soft jelly cast on her that we'll change every forty-eight hours, and we'll X-ray her again in thirty days and take a look."

I put my notebook away. "There's still talk of her as Horse of the Year," I said. "She was easily the most spectacular *performer*."

Frank grinned and nodded. "I appreciate that," he said. "I'd like to see her as Horse of the Year. What she did, she did very impressively."

Three hours later, in his own virtuoso performance, Foolish Pleasure raced to a six-length victory in the Champagne, his last start of the season, and trainer Jolley immediately announced that the colt would be wintering on a farm in Virginia. "Even though he hasn't been hard-raced, sometimes enough is enough," he said as he headed back to the barn. "He's gentle and he's kind; he makes this job easy for me, and we just feel he has done enough. He could win more money this year, but he couldn't gain any more prestige than he already has. In about ten days, we'll turn him out on the farm and let him grow up to be a three-year-old."

Only one filly in history had ever won the Kentucky Derby and that was fully sixty years before, when a lovely candy dish named Regret took the roses in 1915, and here now was an amazon who clearly owned the gifts to pull it off. The thought of Ruffian and Foolish Pleasure hooking up at Churchill Downs on May 3 was irresistible, and I ended my discourse in the October 12 issue of *The Thoroughbred Record* on this sanguine note: "Maybe next year they'll meet—ah, yes, and for the first time in the starting gate at Churchill Downs, in a delayed Champagne at 1¼ miles on the first Saturday in May."

Ruffian did not make it to the Downs that spring.

. . . . . . . . . . . . . . . . .

Late on the Wednesday afternoon of April 30, 1975, as I was fiddling to find a lead for my next day's story, I left my seat in the press box at Churchill Downs and walked to the bank of telephones that lined the back wall. I felt nervous, jumpy, momentarily displaced. I looked at my watch. Ruffian had just finished running in the Comely Stakes at Aqueduct, a seven-eighths of a mile sprint against four nondescript fillies, and I did not see it because I was here instead of there. Whatever else was happening in thoroughbred racing in America, she was the biggest story, the one you knew you would be telling as long as you had breath.

I was in River City to cover Saturday's 101st running of the Derby, a renewal to which Foolish Pleasure was heading as favorite over a herd of largely anonymous manes and tails. His was a status hard earned in the harshest war zones of winter racing for three-year-olds. The bay colt had been in serious training since January, and Jolley had him tight as wire as early as February 12, when he powered through seven-eighths of a mile in 1:21²⁄₅ at Hialeah Park, in Florida, beating two otherwise warm bodies by 4½ lengths. That was hardly more than a stretching exercise compared to what LeRoy had in store for him. The grind began on March 1, when the horse came rushing off the pace to win the 1⅛-mile Flamingo Stakes at Hialeah in the sharp time of 1:48⁴⁄₅. A month later, looking too lightly trained, he finished a

Foolish Pleasure at Churchill Downs

tiring third in the one-mile Florida Derby at Gulfstream Park, but three weeks after that he came roaring back in the Wood Memorial at Aqueduct. He just got up to win it by a head, and this despite the fact that he had broken from the number fifteen post position at the Big A, way out there by the clubhouse mustard stand, and lost several lengths while running outside of horses parked round the first turn. Foolish Pleasure did not have Ruffian's raw ability, nor any of her duende and flare, but he had a kind of terrier courage and toughness that played well in blue-collar Louisville and Queens. In a way, he was a slightly smaller version of his maternal grandsire, the great Tom Fool, and not only in his muscular good looks, but also in his tenacity and resolve. Tom Fool's regular rider, Ted Atkinson, once told me, "When a horse came up along Tom's side, challenging him, I could feel him lower himself as he dug in, and when things got real tight, I could hear him growl." Foolish Pleasure was a growler. He had run three major nine-furlong races in seven weeks, and this enervating regimen brought him to Louisville as fit as a Canadian goose winging into Hilton Head, landing gear down, in November.

While he was touring Florida and New York, Ruffian was on a far softer course. Whiteley had brought her back to the Big Apple that spring to run in the so-called Filly Triple Crown—a far easier counterpart to the more famous Derby-Preakness-Belmont challenge—and the only question was how he would get her to the first leg, the Acorn Stakes, on May 10. There was some chatter that he would enter her in a sprint called the Prioress Stakes, but he never did. He was playing the Fox of Laurel again, saying nothing to tip his hand, until one day he dropped her name into the entry box for a little $20,000 allowance race, the six-furlong Caltha Purse, to be run on April 14. I had not seen her since the day of the Champagne six months before, and so I showed up at Aqueduct in my wheezing green Toyota, not knowing what shape she was in or how she had fared the winter in South Carolina.

Of all the memories I have of Ruffian, few are more vivid than the one of her stepping into the paddock for that otherwise meaningless overnight purse. She came to us that day looking coffee-black and unusually sleek, as if she had been polished by chamois, and her eyes were dark and quick as a robin's blinking at the florisugent crowds. Turning in her paddock stall, she stopped and stood quietly and raised her head and stared off in the distance, as statuesquely beautiful as any horse that I had ever seen—bigger than she was the year before, wider, taller, longer, and more striking to the eye than ever, if that was possible, looking every hand a champion. I saw John Nerud, the trainer of Dr. Fager, leaning on the rail above the saddling paddock, and slipped in next to him.

"A beautiful mare," Nerud said. "Just magnificent."

I then saw something rarely seen in Gotham—a whole battalion of hard-nosed New York horseplayers, the most cynical of their species, erupting into spontaneous applause as the filly left the paddock and rose on the cinder incline to the track. There was a sense of gusting excitement in the air, the promise of a new beginning to the old drama that had been Ruffian. One man called after Whiteley as he strode by.

"What's it like to have a freak of nature?" he asked.

I left the paddock and walked among the bettors who had gathered three-deep around the rail. There was a Brooklyn guy, Jim Toscano, who was there when she won the Astoria. "She won by nine!" Toscano said. "I got $100 to win on her now. She'll win easy. Look at her! *Look at how big she is!*"

There was Mike Abrams, another Brooklyn player, who had come to watch her run. "She looks super," he said. "This is going to be just a workout for her."

They had all admired her last year and now they were back to see history made. Joe Catalano was watching her dance in the post parade. "I'm going to crawl out on a limb," said Joe. "But I think she's the best filly that ever ran."

The Caltha was barely a race. Ruffian left the gate like she was leaving a burning barn. Whiteley had told Vasquez that he didn't want her setting any records, when she got to the front he should just fold up and cruise on her around the turn. She was two in front at the eighth pole when Vasquez decided to ask for just a small burst of speed. He put his hands forward an inch. She got the signal and spurted away. She opened three lengths. Four. Five. Vasquez took a hold and she won it in a common gallop.

Now it was two weeks later and I was in the press box at Churchill calling the aerie at Aqueduct. I got John Pricci, my *Newsday* colleague, on the phone, and asked him, "How'd Ruffian do today?"

He laughed. "What do you think? No contest. She left the gate slow but got it together fast. Went to the lead right away. Won as she pleased. Vasquez never moved. Sound familiar? The sun rises. The sun sets. Ruffian wins by eight."

"How fast?" I asked.

"Very fast," he said. "Stakes record. Seven-eighths in 1:21⅕."

I started to sign off. "Hey, John, Saigon fell today. The war's over."

"Yeah, I know. You were there, weren't you?"

"A year. I went over as an infantry lieutenant trained to lead a platoon into combat. Journalism saved me. I rode a desk right through the Tet offensive. What a fucking waste. But I left a calling card. Just think, John: Right now there's a VC colonel over there listening to Damascus win the Travers by twenty-two."

"What the hell are you talking about?"

"Forget it," I said.

Three days later, Vasquez took Foolish Pleasure in hand out of the gate, allowing him to relax far off Bombay Duck's hot early pace, threaded the colt forward on the rail as they raced down the backstretch for the far turn, deftly split two horses as they moved with a rush on the turn for home, then reined him to the outside in the stretch, looking for room, and drove past the tiring leaders in the last two hundred yards to win the Kentucky Derby by almost two lengths.

Now events began unfolding just as rapidly, leading to that overwhelming question: Could Ruffian beat Foolish Pleasure? The world of the blooded horse turns ever faster in the spring, beginning with the Derby and the race to the Triple Crown, but this time there were two clocks running simultaneously. In fact, the whole show was beginning to feel like a two-ring country carnival and I like just another carnie barker. There I was, at age thirty-four, charging around with my calliope from one tent to the other and back again, trying to keep pace with things. I came home from Louisville on Sunday, and on the ensuing Saturday, May 10, I was slouched in a box seat at Aqueduct as Ruffian appeared for the Acorn. There were rumors everywhere that, if she won that day, Frank would take her straight to Pimlico to meet Foolish Pleasure in the 1³⁄₁₆-mile Preakness Stakes on May 17. It sounded insane to me, so very unlike anything that Whiteley would ever entertain, but it had a seductive reasoning to it. The Janneys were from Maryland, their farm not far from Pimlico, and they had never won the Preakness, their hometown classic. Whiteley fervently denied that he had any plans to ship her to Pimlico. The rumors were like mushrooms. They sprang up overnight. When one wilted in the heat of his denial, another grew in its place— Whiteley was going to run her against the second-string colts in the Withers Mile, and from there, send her against the colts in the Belmont Stakes on June 7.

The fact that Ruffian had become the center of swirling rumors that she was about to step from her division and do battle with the boys was a testimony as to how badly racing's denizens wanted her to do just that. It was a testimony to the flights of imagination that she inspired in those who so steadfastly believed in her and her phenomenal gifts. Like all racetrack rumors of this nature, the strength of their appeal had nothing to do with how factual or ridiculous they might have been; rather they expressed a collective, unconscious yearning for a wish to come true—as a kind of self-fulfilling prophecy. The rumors were everywhere on Acorn day, like the pigeons roosting in the Belmont eaves, elusive and remote, untouchable and untraceable. No matter. Oblivious to all of them, aloof and untouchable in her own detached way, Ruffian showed up for the mile event looking more relaxed and composed than she had for the Caltha. The sheen of her coat fairly mirrored light, and I looked at her more closely than ever as Frank fitted the saddle on her back. For the May 17 issue of *The Thoroughbred Record*, reporting what I saw, I did a couple of cartwheels round the typewriter: "While her shoulders and forearms are elaborately muscled, as are her hindquarters and gaskins, what fills the eye at once is the picture of balance she conveys. She is a study in symmetry. Ruffian moves like an athlete, too, and her ears play constantly among the crowds, as if she were trying to listen to three conversations at once."

The Acorn was an issue never in doubt, though the race left Vasquez decidedly troubled by Ruffian's all-out, grab-the-bit impetuosity. Bouncing to the lead, she relaxed at once in the run from the mile chute down the backside, moving very much within herself as Vasquez, rocking on her back, never so much as twitched. Jockey Ron Turcotte, on the long shot Piece of Luck, thought he would take a peek at what Ruffian had, so he asked his filly for more speed and she moved to Ruffian's flanks. The veteran Turcotte, Secretariat's regular rider, looked over at Ruffian and thought she might be having an off day because she was not fighting Vasquez. "From what I had seen of Ruffian in her other races, she would pull Jacinto to the lead," Turcotte said. "She was so relaxed today. That's when I thought she might be off. It wasn't like her to relax and let me run alongside of her."

Curiously, Vasquez did not feel what Turcotte thought he saw. The moment Piece of Luck ranged next to her, Ruffian came into the bridle and took off. Vasquez could not restrain her. She was a female Dr. Fager, if you must know, the horse that Charles Hatton had once described as "bold and arrogant, conceited and impetuous." She was all of that, to be sure, just sailing along out there as if she owned the place and everybody in it. All poor Jacinto could do was drop his hands and take a long hold and try to get her to settle, but she tooled around Aqueduct that afternoon through a rapid three-quarters of a mile in a zinging 1:09³/₅. She was seven in front with two hundred yards to go and 8¼ lengths in front as she flashed under the wire, in hand the last one hundred yards, in 1:34²/₅, a stakes record. I caught up with Vasquez in the jock's room after I'd talked to Turcotte and told him what Ron had said about how relaxed Ruffian appeared when he came to her side on Piece of Luck. Jacinto shook his head.

"That other filly came alongside and Ruffian got a little rank with me," Jacinto said. And then he added, in frustration, "*She's got to learn to relax!*" I see him now looking tired and vaguely uneasy as we spoke. Asked if he thought she could handle longer distances, he said, "Against these fillies, she could win going two miles."

"Against the colts?"

He shrugged. "These colts are a different story," Jacinto said. "There are five or six colts who can run."

The very next Saturday, in the homestretch of the Preakness at Old Hilltop, Vasquez ran smack into one of them, a lissome chestnut colt named Master Derby. Coming from off the pace, as usual, Foolish Pleasure swung between horses off the last turn and appeared to be making a winning move when, suddenly, front-running Master Derby drifted out and into Pleasure's path. Vasquez hauled left, toward the rail. He was three lengths behind the leader, in the clear, but could whittle that down to no closer than a length before running out of ground. Vasquez cried interference in the stretch run, a reasonable objection, but the stewards waved Master Derby safe at home. There would be no Triple Crown winner in 1975.

The only horse going for a sweep now was Ruffian and this against a bevy of fillies whose ranks she had long ago left in ruins. As spring somersaulted into summer, she seemed to grow only more powerful, dominating her coevals as no other filly in America ever had. Ever since Hot n Nasty had tested her in the Sorority a year before, when she was not really herself, Ruffian had turned her races into mere one-act enter-tainments, bloodless exhibitions of her prodigal speed. That she was beating very little did not discourage those who came to watch her work. Nothing fires the imagination of the racing world faster than an animal with blinding lick. Speed is the very essence of the thoroughbred, the golden spring that makes the clock go tick, and Ruffian expressed the essence as it was rarely done; not once, but time and time again. She flew through eleven-second eighths with ferocious regularity, parboiling her fastest rivals through strings of them—:11, :22, :33, :44—and she owned stakes records in every major event in which she had run. Life for her was a tern in a breeze—twelve quarts of oats, a can of sweet feed, and five-eighths in :58.

Two weeks after Foolish Pleasure lost the Preakness, in a moment buoyed and blessed by Whiteley's refreshing understatement, Jacinto Vasquez jumped off Ruffian in the immediate wake of the Mother Goose Stakes, weighed himself out on the Aqueduct jockey scales, and stepped across the cinders to greet Stuart Janney and his trainer.

"Beautiful, Jacinto, beautiful," said Stuart.

In a flicker of a smile, Jacinto said to Whiteley, "How did we play this game?"

Whiteley fetched up a hayseed grin he'd first learned over in Centreville. "You didn't do too bad," he said.

Ruffian had just answered a question that had lingered in the air since she had won the Fashion Stakes a year ago. Her pedigree was so shot through with speed, with all that Bold Ruler and Native Dancer blood coursing through her veins—and she ran so damn fast from flag fall to finish—that suspicions about her stamina tracked her like a vapor wherever she raced and whenever people talked about her. What deepened those suspicions was the bold, headstrong way she had of going, the Dr. Fagering we'd seen as recently as the Acorn. The 1⅛-mile Mother Goose would be Ruffian's first adventure traveling a middle distance of ground, her first time racing around two turns. Whiteley had been working hard at harnessing her phenomenal energies, at getting her to settle down. In the paddock before the Mother Goose, he told Jacinto, "Take a *long* hold of her. Don't choke her. Try to get her to relax."

The Mother Goose was all that Frank could have devoutly wished. Out of the gate, Ruffian rolled monotonously to the lead and just kept going. Jacinto did what he was told. Taking a long hold, his feet on the dash, he just sat there while Ruffian tooled around the first turn, opening a length-and-a-half lead on Sun and Snow, running slower than she'd ever run in all her life, and then all eyes swung to the Teletimer as it flashed and froze in lights a quarter-mile split never seen in a Ruffian race: :24⅕. Taking a long hold on his cigarette, Whiteley appeared as relaxed as Ruffian. Six horses followed her down the backstretch, looking like ducklings chasing after Mother. None dared to challenge her. None dared to force the issue. Dan's Commander, jockey Rudy Turcotte up, had tripped and fallen next to Ruffian at the start, dashing Rudy to the dirt and nearly knocking him out, drawing a gasp from the railbird crowds. Vasquez had seen her go down and watched the riderless filly as she toured Queens along the outside fence. Behind him, the gate crew swept up a dazed Rudy, cradling him in their arms, and bore him away like a fallen charioteer. None of this had affected Ruffian. There she was, galloping easily along the backside straight, Vasquez leaning back and rocking in this hammock of a wind she was creating for him at the half-mile pole. There the timer flashed its friendly message: :47⅗, by nearly two full seconds the slowest she had ever raced a half-mile in her life.

Vasquez was elated. "Ruffian was running beautiful, under command, entirely relaxed," he said. "She was cookin' and lookin'."

At once Sir Ivor's Sorrow moved to Ruffian's flank. Ruffian barely noticed. Jacinto took another hold of her and got the horse to switch her leads from right foreleg to left and she took off. She opened two lengths at the point of the last turn. She opened three. Four. Five at the top of the stretch. He did not want her too relaxed. "She was going to have to meet tougher competition than these," he said. Coming to midstretch, Vasquez started pumping his hands and tapping her lightly on the shoulder with his stick. She quickened through the lane. Six in front. Seven. Eight. Nine. Ten. By the time she swept under the wire, 13½ lengths in front, even the most skeptical of horseplayers were on their feet and giving her a standing O. She broke the stakes record, nine furlongs in 1:47⅘, only four-fifths of a second off the gifted Riva Ridge's track record.

I wandered down to the racetrack and was standing there when Vasquez got off and went to Janney and Whiteley. Testy as usual, impatient with ceremony—"Let's get it over with"—Whiteley got into the bit on his way back to the barn and played back her performance in the key of low. "She did all right," he said. "She beat a bad bunch … This is the farthest that she's ever been, and I didn't know how she was going to get the last eighth. She went a mile and an eighth against these horses all right. We'll wait and see."

Thing is, Frank Whiteley was absolutely right. She had not beaten much. She had run very fast again, farther than ever, but among these scrawny-assed fillies, these ear-twirlers with big eyes and long lashes, Ruffian stood out like a she-bear roaming around a den of cubs. So what was the point of this exercise? Worse than monotonous, Ruffian's exertions were beginning to verge on the boring. Leaving the ceremony that day, I could only imagine what was going to happen next. The Coaching Club

American Oaks, at a mile and a half, was three weeks away, and under ordinary circumstances, with a high-class filly, the natural and prudent thing to do would be to saddle her up and complete the sweep for the Triple Crown. Alas, these were not normal times, and Ruffian was not just another high-class filly. She was vastly more charismatic and gifted than any of the last three thoroughbreds to win the Filly Triple—Dark Mirage (1968), Shuvee (1969) and Chris Evert (1974)—and there were reasonable people on the grounds saying that she might be the greatest female racehorse of all time, better than Twilight Tear and Bewitch, better than Gallorette and Busher, better than Artful and Regret. The Belmont Stakes was only seven days after the Mother Goose, but Ruffian had not been hard-raced and surely, with the easy Acorn and the Mother Goose in her tank, she might just drumroll to the lead in the Belmont, prick her ears and pick up the beat, and simply dare any of those foolish colts to come join her. Foolish Pleasure? He wouldn't dare. Run with Ruffian? Are you crazy? Trying to run with her would only set it up for Master Derby or Avatar, who finished second in the Kentucky Derby, or any other stretch-runner hoping to catch wet sails down that long Belmont stretch.

So, at the end of yet another chase, I asked Frank, "How about the Belmont Stakes?"

Whiteley shot me a look. "What in the hell would I do that for?" he asked.

"Then what?"

"Probably the Oaks," he said, striding away. "I'll have to talk to Mr. Janney."

Turning back, I slipped into the jock's room at the foot of the stairs.

Inside, wiping his face with a towel, Vasquez looked wonderfully relieved. "What about the mile and a half of the Oaks?" I asked him.

"Distance isn't going to make any difference," he said. "She can go ten miles."

On June 7, in as furious a finish as I had witnessed in the Belmont Stakes, Avatar held off a charging Foolish Pleasure to win by a neck. Master Derby came in third. I was standing on the crown of the racetrack when Bill Shoemaker brought Avatar back to get his picture taken. It had been twenty years since he had brought Swaps to the rail at Washington Park and he was forty-three now, but finessing horses through traffic as well as ever and his sense of timing seemed as sharp as it was when he was flying around those ovals outside Chicago. Avatar's trainer, Tommy Doyle, came forward onto the crown and looked up at The Shoe, who blurted: "He run a hell of a race, Tommy!"

"Thank you, Bill, thank you! You rode a super race. It was a super ride!"

The next morning, with the horse barely cooled out, Doyle put Avatar on a plane at John F. Kennedy International Airport and spirited him home to California.

..................

The pace of things began to quicken even more through early June. A day after Avatar fled town, the New York Racing Association, which runs the tracks at Belmont, Aqueduct and Saratoga, offered the largest purse in the sport's history, $300,000, for a contest matching the winners of the three Triple Crown races—Foolish Pleasure, Master Derby and Avatar. All you had to do was walk into Belmont to hear the horse-players singing in chorus: "What about Ruffian?" For reasons still murky to me, they had left her out, even though Whiteley had expressed an interest in running her for what he called "that kind of money." Jack Dreyfus, the chairman of the New York Racing Association and founder of the Dreyfus Fund, explained her absence: "Ruffian is another game for another time. First we have to decide the colt championship." Jolley soon agreed and so did Master Derby's trainer, Smiley Adams, but Doyle did not want to fly Avatar back across the country. He declined.

I could see where this was going and suddenly there it went. When Avatar defected, the filly who had just been excluded as another game for another time was invited to join the Derby and Preakness winners in a three-horse match, but here LeRoy Jolley's brains got the better of him and he hesitated. Lee had been around the racetrack all his life; his father Moody was a leading trainer too, and he could see it all unfolding now on the mile-and-a-quarter chute at Belmont Park:

*Ruffian sails to an uncontested lead, Vasquez taking a long hold and getting her to relax, while Baeza and Foolish Pleasure sit back with McHargue and Master Derby. What other choice do McHargue and Baeza have? Who would elect to hook the buzz saw on the front end? If Baeza goes charging to her flanks to force a realistic pace, he only sets it up for McHargue and a late-charging Master Derby. If McHargue elects to prompt her, Baeza waits behind with Foolish Pleasure and pounces on the turn for home. So Ruffian gets a half-mile in :47 and is two in front and alas it is too late to catch her.*

A match race, yes, Jolley said. A three-horse race, no.

Desperate for a marquee event to enliven interest in a waning sport, the NYRA pooh-bahs hatched the only extravaganza left to them. They gave the owner of Master Derby, Mrs. Robert Lehman, $50,000 in disappearance money. She took it and went quietly away. You just knew that Frank Whiteley did not like the idea, but he came under pressure from the Janneys. The single biggest power in New York racing was the Phipps family, Ogden the elder and his son, Ogden Mills, who was known by everyone as Dinny. Of course, since Stuart was married to Ogden's sister, Ruffian was a member by extension of that family, and Whiteley knew that Stuart was being urged by his brother-in-law to run her. The sport needed her. It needed her box-office appeal, her starshine. She had become a kind of national pet, as famous horses do in this land, and Foolish Pleasure owned this hard-earned image as a gritty little rough-neck of a colt who walked with a swagger and took no shit from any man's horse. He was Vasquez with a fur coat. So it came about that Jolley and a reluctant Whiteley agreed to a $350,000 match race between Ruffian and Foolish Pleasure, $225,000 to the winner and $125,000 to the loser: a mile and a quarter, out of that little-used backstretch chute, on Sunday, July 6.

Foolish Pleasure was done with racing for the moment, but Ruffian still had that watered-down Filly Triple Crown to sweep. The $100,000 added Coaching Club American Oaks on June 21 was a full three-eighths of a mile farther than the Mother Goose and Ruffian was running as if distances did not matter, but a race at a mile and a half holds a searching light to a horse's heart and I was thinking foolishly that she might get on the muscle and win by twenty and challenge Secretariat's world mark of 2:24 flat.

I joined LeRoy Jolley in the paddock and walked up the winding staircase to the box seat section with him. He was heading for his seat, his binoculars swinging from his hand.

"Mind if I join you?" I asked.

"Not at all," he said.

We settled in a box not far from where the Janneys and Whiteley were sitting. Frank ate another Gelusil and stepped on his cigarette. The calmest creature in the whole place was Ruffian, who quietly entered the backdoor of post position five and left through the front door with a rush, at once galloping to the sunlight on the first turn and opening five lengths through a casual opening quarter. She relaxed even more down the backstretch through a half-mile in :49 flat, a canter in the park for her, while Jolley kept his glasses trained on her. It is more than six hundred yards across that vast infield and she looked like a stick figure out there, a little metronome going tick-tock-tick-tock along that lofty stand of trees.

"How's she look out there?" I asked.

"Very easy, she's just galloping," said Jolley. At the far turn, emboldened by the slow pace, Equal Change and Let Me Linger ran up on either side of Ruffian and there was an audible gasp from the crowd. Ruffian pricked her ears as the interlopers came to her, as if she were happy for the company, but moments later she spurted away, opening three lengths on the turn for home. Vasquez never twitched, riding her with utter confidence all the way home. She cantered by us in hand again, to ovations that rippled all through the grandstand and the clubhouse, and Jolley lowered his glasses and watched in silence as she galloped out to the first turn.

"What do you think?" I asked.

"She's very, very tough," he said. "She did what she had to do ... " Lee took off through the clubhouse crowd, weaving in and out of knots of gamblers, and stepped onto the escalator to the ground level. He was heading back to his barn to check on Foolish Pleasure. "It takes a game horse to go a mile and a half on the lead like that," he said. "I don't think Jacinto ever hit her. She was under a hold all the way and she was in front all the way. That's her game. She *makes* that her game."

"How do you plan to run against her?"

"There's only one way to run *against* her," he said softly, "and that's to run *with* her."

Foolish Pleasure had recently turned in a fiery workout at Belmont Park, the first stage in Jolley's plan to make the colt stiletto sharp for the match. I remarked to him about that workout.

Jolley smiled. "He has speed if he needs it," he said.

He was winding along a path around the paddock. "I really feel, very sincerely, that you're going to see a real battle in that match race," Jolley said. "She doesn't give up and neither does he."

He came to the tunnel leading to shed row. Funny Cat, the filly who had finished last in the Oaks, was panting hotly as she strode by. Groom Elish Smith was holding fast to the reins of her bridle. He spotted LeRoy. "Mr. Jolley!" cried Elish. "It's all up to you. You and The Pleasure have to get her. It's all up to you now."

"Nobody's got her yet!" Jolley said.

"That's why it's up to you!" Elish said.

Moments later the trainer was stepping into the cool dimness of his shed and heading towards Foolish Pleasure's stall. The Pleasure's exercise rider, John Nazareth, greeted him there.

John was complaining that the other six fillies in the Oaks had let her run loose on the front end. "They all gave her a chance, letting her gallop out there on the lead," John said to Lee.

LeRoy shook his head. "But any horse who goes with her dies like a dog," he said.

In his stall, The Pleasure was nibbling from a rack of hay, looking sleek and muscular and paying no mind to the men outside his door who spoke of Ruffian. Jolley went over and patted the colt on the nose. "It's going to be a contest," Jolley said. "Neither is going to be a pushover."

. . . . . . . . . . . . . . . . .

I am sorting now through old scraps of paper, soiled by mustard stains, browned with age, looking for where it all went haywire, searching for the exit where I leaped from the Great Match Race circus wagon that June. All I remember is that I ended up sitting in Dick Sandler's office at *Newsday* and telling him I wanted out. I had no darksome premonitions about what might happen on July 6, but I did have a sense of anxiety, feelings rooted in my own unpleasant experience with the Swaps-Nashua match twenty years before, and I told him how that race had left me gun-shy about matches, about how they always ended up looking like cartoons, gross exaggerations that did not mirror true ability: Seabiscuit-War Admiral. Armed-Assault. Chris Evert-Miss Musket. Swaps-Nashua. They were all pressure and no pace. Worse, Ruffian-Foolish Pleasure had taken on an added starter that seemed to grow more wretched every day: a phony, circuslike atmosphere created around the marketing gimmick that the race had something to do with the newly emergent women's liberation movement. So it became boy versus girl, what the marketers were exploiting as "The Great Battle of the Sexes," a hyped-up sales job that involved refrying some very old and tasteless beans. That is, it became another variation of the cartoonish 1973 tennis match between the aging Billie Jean King and golden oldie Bobby Riggs, only this time with manes and tails.

So, the week before the Great Match Race, I left Long Island with the New York Yankees, took off but never really left Belmont Park behind. I kept in close and constant touch with what was happening there. In the week before the race, Ruffian worked a blistering five-eighths in :58⅕ on the main track. Whiteley was winding her like a watch. Foolish Pleasure had worked very slowly a few days earlier, six furlongs in a hoof-dragging 1:14, and Jolley was so distraught by the languor of the move that he threw up his breakfast on the side of his barn. LeRoy knew that Foolish Pleasure, if he had any chance to stay with Ruffian, any chance at all, would have to work much faster than that. The reason for this is simple: In the final days leading up to longer races, such as the mile-and-a-quarter Kentucky Derby, fast workouts over short distances are generally seen as essential to success. They are known in the training game as "zingers" or "sharpeners," and they work to bring these already high-strung thoroughbreds to a very fine edge, to hone and sharpen their speed, to bring them to their toes. Everybody in the racing business knew that the classic match race—as epitomized by Seabiscuit-War Admiral or Swaps-Nashua—is invariably won by the horse who flashes the most speed out of the gate, who grabs the lead at the git-go and plays catch-me-if-you-can. Knowing that Foolish Pleasure's final work was far too slow to prepare him to do that, especially against a horse as fast as Ruffian, Jolley saddled the colt for one final zinger at Belmont Park.

What Foolish Pleasure did that morning is remembered as no more than a foot-note today, but it turned out to be a pivotal moment in the annals of the turf, certainly in the history of American match races. In one of the most brilliant workouts ever witnessed at Belmont Park, the colt bounded through five-eighths of a mile in :56²/₅, two-fifths of a second faster than Secretariat had worked the same distance so brilliantly two years earlier, when he was drilling for his victory in the Man o' War Stakes. Foolish Pleasure's workout left the clockers gasping, checking their watches with each other, and it immediately put me in mind of one other highly sensational move leading up to a mile-and-a-quarter match race: Nashua's equally fast workout at Saratoga, on the deep training track known as Oklahoma, on the eve of his departure to Chicago to meet Swaps in their celebrated set-to.

Though Ruffian was favored, many veteran handicappers began to see the colt as the horse who would take the most beating. Foolish Pleasure's one major advantage coming to the race involved the brutal nature of his campaign as compared to hers. He had been in hard and serious training since the first of the year, and for four long months—from his victory in the nine-furlong Flamingo Stakes at Hialeah, on March 1—he had been battle-hardened under the sternest trials that the sport can offer. Since the Flamingo, he had won the Wood and the Kentucky Derby and had never been worse than third against the best colts that could be marshaled against him. Ruffian was anything but battle-hardened. She was so superior to her female counter-parts, so much faster, that she had never been truly tested, and there was a lingering sense she'd had it so easy in her career as a racehorse that she might wilt under the kind of heat that Foolish Pleasure was capable of generating. Ruffian was the greatest filly I had ever seen, and clearly the sentimental favorite with the crowds, but anybody paying attention knew that she would be facing a battle-scarred opponent who was coming to the race as sharp as he had ever been in his life. His final workout was the red flag signaling his heated intentions. It announced to the racing world that he would be coming to the post on the muscle, his eyes bulging, and that Ruffian would have to run harder and faster than she'd ever had to run in her life, that she would be pressured and tested as she'd never been before, that her days of cruising on easy and uncontested leads were over now and she would have to fight for ground each step of the way.

. . . . . . . . . . . . . . . . .

The distant memory's a ghostly thing, a Wisconsin meadow of lost time black as pitch, with only here and there some little necklaced pools of light leading nowhere, scattered about. The news clippings help, but I have no memory of when I got home that week, and the next thing I remember somewhat vaguely is this: I am sitting with some reporters in a box seat at Belmont near Dick Sandler and his wife, Gloria, and my wife and Nick and Eileen Sordi, our friends, while Ruffian and Foolish Pleasure are walking to the gate at the end of the mile-and-a-quarter chute. It looks five miles away.

It is late Sunday afternoon, and CBS-TV cameras are keeping an eye on the place for the millions who have tuned in. Music is playing and 50,764 people are milling around in T-shirts that say either "I'm for Foolish Pleasure" or "I'm For Ruffian," and many are wearing metal pins bearing his picture or her picture and they are waiting now draped along the apron fence or folded in their seats. They are laughing and talking, drinking and arguing. The Great Match Race has become a transcending event, national in scope, which has engaged and connected more people with thoroughbred racing than has happened at any time in the sport's history. Though it has nothing whatever to do with the women's movement, the match has come to resonate for many as a symbol of the struggle between the sexes; for millions of women, Ruffian has come to represent the newly ascendant female taking the fight to a male-dominated world. It is a fantasy that has crossed gender lines and now appeals to men and women on both sides.

This ignored the inconvenient fact that whole generations of gifted female runners had long been waging successful war against their male counterparts. The great female Gallorette had made a living pounding on such established males as Stymie and Pavot, and did not the great filly Busher once beat up on the mighty gelding Armed? Did not young Askmenow defeat the legendary Count Fleet? And did not the decidedly feminine Bewitch once beat Citation? And did not Twilight Tear, one of the fastest females of all time, twice make easy pickings of Kentucky Derby winner Pensive, a colt, then crush the hard-charging older horse, Devil Diver, in the '44 Pimlico Special, beating him by six widening lengths? None of that seemed to matter now. In the race that would settle the male-female question once and for all time, Ruffian was girding to take on Foolish Pleasure in the decisive combat between the genders.

Sitting there at Belmont on the day of the Great Match Race, I peel back the onion of the *Daily Racing Form* and turn to Ruffian's past performances. As printed there, her PPs constitute a visual of numbers as rare as she: at every pole, at every race she has ever been in, there is the number "1," indicating that she has never been behind a horse at any point of call at any time in ten lifetime starts. I'd never seen a PP line remotely like it, not even in Man o War's nearly singular PPs. *The New York Times* has printed a graphic of the type normally seen before prizefights, with the height indicating the point of the withers on the back:

## Tale of the Tape

|           | RUFFIAN          | FOOLISH PLEASURE  |
|-----------|------------------|-------------------|
| Age       | 3                | 3                 |
| Sex       | Filly            | Colt              |
| Bred      | Kentucky         | Florida           |
| Color     | Dark Bay         | Bay               |
| Weight    | 1,125 pounds     | 1,061             |
| Height    | 5 ft. 3 in.      | 5 ft. 3¼ in.      |
| Girth     | 6 ft. 3½ in.     | 6 ft. 1 in.       |
| Impost    | 121 pounds       | 126 pounds        |
| Shoe Size | 5                | 6                 |

I set the paper down, fidgeting and shifting in my seat. Big races, big fights and the Indianapolis 500 would always fill me with nausea and unleavened dread, as dangerous to life as they are, but this match race is worse than most because it is drawing too from that old abandoned well, to the point that again I am having trouble with my binoculars. I have my field glasses with me this time and I raise them to my eyes as Ruffian and Foolish Pleasure disappear around the back of the starting gate, but my hands, like Red Smith's, have always shaken so badly at times like this that I can see nothing through them. I hand them to Dick and we wait.

It lasts only forty-five seconds. Starter George Cassidy springs the latch and they vault from the gate, Ruffian on the inside, Foolish Pleasure on the outside, but she has hit the right side of her stall as she comes away and Foolish Pleasure breaks a half-length in front and is gathering speed quickly down the chute. At once the filly begins to bear out, as though she might be feeling some discomfort from striking the gate, and she begins to lean into Foolish Pleasure and herd him towards the crown of the track. The stewards see this from their aerie, but the horses are too far away for me to see what is happening and all I remember is hearing the din of the crowds erupting all around and seeing the blur of two horses running almost as a team along the chute, driving towards the main track. Now they are coming into clearer view. Vasquez is asking Ruffian to make up the half a length she lost at the break, his hands are pumping on her, and she is cutting the margin to a neck ... a head ... a half a head.

She comes to him. They are nose to nose. The two of them are hurtling out of the chute and down the long backstretch. She sticks her nose in front of his. She thrusts it to a head. Ruffian freezes the Teletimer at the 440-yard mark at :22⅕. I did not know this then, but that split is a sizzler coming from that deeper, unused chute and she hits the main track flying. Foolish Pleasure clings to her, not letting her get away, not letting her get loose on the lead as she has been loose all these months and races past. All down the backstretch she is bearing out on the colt until she extends her lead to a long head and then a neck and finally, seven hundred yards from the barrier, she is a full half-length in front and looking like she might finally pry herself loose from Foolish Pleasure when that grazing pigeon suddenly flew up in front of them and Vasquez and Baeza heard the loud snap, like a dead stick cracking in two, and Ruffian suddenly sags right, bumping into the colt. He flies from her side and she struggles to stay with him and even runs spastically another forty yards, driving her injured leg into the ground as she keens in pain and panic to the outside hedge. Vasquez strains to pull her up. She bobbles once more and halts. Vasquez immediately jumps off her back and holds the reins awaiting help.

The instant she stops running, I am gone. I race down the long box-seat aisle and bound down the winding stairs, two at a time, to the tunnel that runs from the paddock to the main track. At the end of the tunnel I emerge into the eerie church-like silence that has fallen across the place. I glance up at the stands. Hands are holding faces, heads are down, and I look across the track and can see where she is standing seven hundred yards away. I bend over and start to slip under the metal pipe that forms the outside rail when a large Pinkerton guard steps in front of me.

"Where do you think you're going?" he asks.

I point over his shoulder. "Over there," I say. "Where that filly just broke down." He glares down at me. "Oh, no you're not! You're not allowed over there."

"You can't stop me!"

I hear a voice behind me and look around. It is Ken Denlinger of *The Washington Post*. "Can I go with ya?" he asks.

Now a half-dozen photographers come charging to the rail, ten feet to our right. The guard sees them and holds up his arms and walks to where they are, waving them back. "No, no, can't go on the track!" I slip under the rail and start across the track right by the finish line. I hear a noise. I look left. It is Baeza yelling at me. He is thundering toward me on the back of Foolish Pleasure. "Hey! Hey!" he screams. I freeze on the crown and feel the cold hairs standing on the back of my neck. Denlinger is behind me. Foolish Pleasure races by and I can feel the wind in his wake as he passes. We take off across the crown of the track. I can hear the guard yelling. "No! Hey, no!" We are gone. Under the inside rail of the dirt course. Under the outside rail of the turf course. Past the tote board on the left. Past the flagpole on the right. Across the boundless stretch of grass. We are running. I can see her standing by the hedge and people swarming around her. I stop and walk, panting in the heat. Run another fifty yards. Slow to a jog. Nearly vomit. Walk thirty yards past a dead grey squirrel. Bend over, drooling. Glimpse the white-and-green horse ambulance pulling slowly to a stop near Ruffian. Head down. Run another seventy yards. Slow to a jog again. Breathing deep and fast. Pick it up again. At last reach the outer rail of the dirt track. There Doc Gilman is kneeling under Ruffian and fitting her with an inflatable plastic cast. He fits it around her lower right front leg. She is in a panic. Beads of sweat are running off her belly. Her large brown eyes are circled in white and robin quick as they dart everywhere, and she tries to stand on the injured leg but it buckles under her and she leaps back and rears up fighting the cast. Gilman reaches for her. A man from the starting gate is holding her reins.

"Whoa, whoa!" says Gilman. "Easy, filly … easy now!"

The mammoth grandstand is silent in the distance and far away but we always must protect the people from their feelings and so an old guy named Horace Blue Rapelyea, the ambulance driver, appears in a scene that is comic noir, coming forward with The Screen but he comes too late. Gilman has secured the cast and now they walk her hobbling terribly into the back of the ambulance, up and in. I look at Gilman. He is standing, his arms akimbo, and has blood on both his hands.

"What happened to her, Doc?" I ask.

"She's shattered both her sesamoids," he says, referring to the small pivot bones, each no bigger than a thumbnail, that are a vital part of the horse's structural system in the ankle, acting as little pulleys for the suspensory ligament. "Right foreleg … "

"But why all the blood?"

"They exploded out of the ankle," he says.

I have seen that injury before and it sounds to me like a sentence of death, but I have to ask, and I know no other way to ask it but clinically, seeking refuge in the coldest of words. "What's the prognosis?"

Doc Gilman says nothing. He shakes his head and walks away. He climbs into the ambulance van.

*Oh no*, I thought. *Ruffian is dead.*

Frank Whiteley arrives in a car. He hops out, a look of utter horror on his face, his lips caked in Gelusil white.

"I want to get in with her," Frank yells.

Gilman leaves the cab and starts to the back of the van. Whiteley sees the delay this will cause and he shouts to Gilman: "You don't have to do that. I'll ride here."

Frank hops onto the joint connecting the cab to the van and they pull away. Over the speed bumps that rib the backstretch roads, around the Frenchman's Kitchen, down into the valley below the kitchen and to the door of Barn 34, Whiteley's barn. They open the back door of the ambulance. Grown men are talking to her like the child she is, coaxing her to turn around and step down, and she limps off the van.

. . . . . . . . . . . . . . . . . .

The scene at the barn that early evening was of a horror beyond any manner of escape or reckoning. Grooms and hotwalkers and trainers came from barns all around this little city of horses and sheds and began their slow descent into the valley towards Whiteley's barn. People were weeping openly. Ruffian was out of the ambulance and standing on three legs and Gilman was bent over checking the cast he had put on at the track. The cast was a crimson ruin. It had ruptured under the expanding pressure of the hemorrhaging wound and was no longer giving her any support. The crushing of the sesamoids, like that of a marble smashed by a hammer, had destroyed the structure that supported her lower leg and that allowed her to flex her foot; bone fragments were driven out the back of the pastern and were protruding there. The foot and fetlock dangled from the nub of the ankle because the string on the kite had broken and she no longer had control of them.

Gilman was holding her right leg off the ground. "Get me another one of these casts," he said. Someone scurried off to look for another cast.

The main veterinarians had arrived. Doc Prendergast, her regular vet, gave her a shot of tranquilizer, and Dr. Alex Harthill from Kentucky was there and they joined Gilman and went to work around her. Newspapermen and newspaperwomen were there with pads and soon the crowds were clustering in a semicircle about fifteen yards around Ruffian. NYRA stableman Frank Tours and a few Pinkerton guards stood in a perimeter around her and the kneeling vets as they worked to treat the wounds. Both ankles were hemorrhaging, the shattered right and also the bottom of the left ankle that had born all her weight and skidded along the track as she hobbled to the outside fence. Barbara Phipps Janney came out of the crowd and walked to Ruffian's left side. Crying, she patted her on the nose and turned and left to join her niece Cynthia, brother Ogden's daughter. Stuart Janney stood off by himself, looking very sad and grave, his Brooks Brothers back leaning up against the barn, his binoculars case hanging from his arm. He had ridden performance horses all of his life, over the most dangerous courses in the world, and he had seen many horses fall and seen many of them hopelessly broken and dying even but he had never witnessed anything to harden him for this. He watched his wife as she came and went and then the men as they crouched working around the filly and then Dan Williams, who months ago had taken Minnor Massey's place as Ruffian's groom, as he stood holding her.

The wound was very dirty and needed badly to be debrided and cleaned to prevent infection but first they had to stop what Harthill kept referring to as "this terrible hemorrhaging." They brought a bucket of ice and set it in front of her. Williams wrapped her damaged foot in a bandage and lowered it into the ice. They had to move fast. Her condition was growing more serious and complicated. The bleeding was one thing. She was also badly dehydrated and slipping into shock. They decided to move her into her stall. She could not walk on the dangling right foot. So Frank's assistant, Mike Bell, held her head. Frank and Dan Williams joined hands under the filly's belly. Doc Harthill and Yates Kennedy joined hands under her rump from behind. They lifted and pulled Ruffian the last ten yards to her stall. She began thrashing and rearing as she slipped deeper into pain and shock and more pain and shock. Her eyes were wild and she was sweating and breathing heavily. I saw Doc Prendergast slip next to her in the stall and begin giving her a series of injections on the *left* side of her neck: first a coagulant to stop the bleeding, then penicillin and a tetanus shot. He gave her Butazolidin, an anti-inflammatory drug, and a pain-killing narcotic called Talwin. They lowered her foot into the bucket of ice. I slipped inside the shed, sidling along the wall opposite from her stall, a fly on the windowsill, and watched while she seemed to settle as the drugs took hold.

Outside the shed Barbara Janney had begun wailing piteously—it still echoes in memory to this day—and nothing Stuart or Cynthia said or did could succor her. And then something happened that would haunt me for years: fast and hard from my left, through the door of the shed, swept a pug-nosed veterinarian named William O. Reed, whose equine hospital was directly across the road. Reed had the plastic protective tip of a hypodermic needle between his teeth and he ducked into Ruffian's stall and stuck the needle in the *right* side of her neck. He emptied the syringe. I looked to my left and right and saw that no one had seen him and I began wondering whether Prendergast knew what Reed had given her and wondering who was running this madhouse, and all the while there came the high-pitched sobbing of that grief-stricken woman just outside the door, Ruffian frightened and trembling as she descended in a spiral of pain and shock, and in a macabre denouement came this uninvited vet stepping into her stall like a thief in the night and ...

Shortly after Reed walked away Ruffian became crazed, like her sire two years later when they tried to fit him with that cast, rising up and nearly toppling over, lashing out with her feet, throwing herself against the wall, trying to heave herself to the ground. I turned away. You could hear the voices shouting from inside the stall. The men in the stall were frantically working to control her.

As Harthill later explained: *The pain became greater with the shock, and this developed into what we call a vicious cycle. The more pain, the more shock; the more shock, the more pain. There were several of us in the stall with her in an attempt to maintain her composure. After a time, the thing became more intensive. She was trying to lie down. We were doing our best to hold her up while instituting ice therapy ... For an hour we did the best we could with ice therapy and taking X-rays. Ruffian became more violent, even with the medications. The shock was going faster than the medications could work ...*

I left the barn and raced back to the press box to write the story, and by the time that job was done, Ruffian had been transported to Reed's hospital on Plainview Avenue and was undergoing surgery. Esposito's bar was across a side street from the hospital and the bar became the center of a vigil that lasted far into the night. I did not wait to hear the reading of the final bulletin. I knew she was doomed, I guess, knew it from what I had already seen and heard that day, knew from watching her the last twelve months that she was too headstrong and opinionated and willful to tolerate anything so confining as a sling or a cast. What would kill her, in the end, was what had made her Ruffian from the beginning. So I climbed into the old Toyota and rattled home to Huntington. They say she died twice on the operating table and that they had to use artificial respiration and stimulants to get her breathing again, to get her massive heart to beating again. They fitted her with a plaster cast and finally lay her in a padded recovery room and waited for her to come to. Ruffian was lying on her side when she came to and opened her eyes. It was as though she had been dreaming of her final moments as a racehorse, of the final forty seconds when she caught Foolish Pleasure and started to leave him, because she woke up running, her hind legs and forelegs pumping and striding out.

The doctors and attendants all kneeled next to her to keep her down, but she started running faster and then thrashing harder, throwing the men around like rag dolls, her thrashings uncontrollable, until finally she broke her elbow with the heavy plaster cast and dislodged the cast from her leg. It started slipping off. They could see that she was hemorrhaging terribly again, and her right leg was greatly swollen from the pounding as she flailed around, and that's when the medical team all came together and shook their heads and told Whiteley that the struggle was over. It was done. They could do no more. Prendergast said to stop. Harthill called Stuart Janney and told him that gangrene was inescapable and it was entirely hopeless. The gentleman from Maryland said, "I'm a realistic man and I have been in the horse business long enough to know you can do so much and that's as far as you can go. Thank everyone very much."

He hung up.

I awoke at 3 a.m. and padded downstairs and out the door to the car. I turned on the radio and spun the dial 'til I heard the news: "Ruffian, the great filly who broke down in a match race yesterday with Foolish Pleasure, was destroyed at 2:20 this morning after undergoing ... "

Click.

Someone called the Janneys from Lexington, Kentucky, and offered to bury her near her birthplace, but Stuart already knew what he wanted to do. He asked that Ruffian be buried at Belmont Park, where she had lived and trained most of her racing life, where she had won her first start by fifteen, where she had won the Acorn and Mother Goose and Oaks, and where she had died on the lead.

Later that Monday, a backhoe was seen chuffing across the infield at Belmont Park. It stopped in front of the association flagpole, just inside the turf course not far from the lake, and began digging the grave, taking large bites of the ground and depositing the dirt on a green mat. By 8 p.m., the digging largely done, a ring of

Pinkerton guards had formed a line along the turf course to keep out intruders and now stable workers were climbing the stairs into the clocker's shed on the clubhouse turn and drifting to the outside fence and standing on the rungs of the ladder leading to the film tower. Finally, the small mourning party arrived: Frank and his son David, Vasquez and Mike Bell, Frank's wife, Louise, and Dan Williams came slowly across the track and moved to where the crane was digging the ten-foot-deep hole in the ground. The Janneys had gone to their place in Maine. Some association officials and a few reporters drifted onto the infield and watched as the gravediggers worked around the hole.

Every now and then, Frank walked to the edge of the grave and looked down inside, then turned away. He was holding a pair of red coolers, large blankets that horses wear when they are cooling out. I was told that I wasn't welcome at the service, that I looked too much like an "ambulance chaser" galloping across the infield, but an association man, Pat O'Brien, had spoken on my behalf and I was invited to join the twenty-five or so people who had gathered there. In the end, workers came and went like ants around the grave, grading the inside of it with spades and shovels.

The sun went down. It grew silent in the dark.

"They say these things happen, but you see them happen and they don't seem real," said Vasquez, almost whispering. "She was a kind filly. It was so easy in the morning to take her to the racetrack and bring her back. Coming off the racetrack, the first thing she would do was look around for some place to graze. She would look for leaves on the trees on the way back. I used to break off the leaves coming back with her to the barn and she would look, turn her neck around and take them. Nothing bothered her. She didn't have a nerve in her body. She was very smart. She'd hear a photographer walking around and she would hear the shutter clicking and she'd raise her head and look at the photographer like, 'Go ahead. Take a picture.'"

The burial ceremony, July 7, 1975

Delivered privately, that was the only eulogy there was.

It was past 9 p.m. by the time the grave was finished and it was dark on the infield when the van bearing Ruffian's remains appeared in the distance, coming across the chute where she and the colt had been hurtling head and head the afternoon before. The headlights grew slowly larger in the distance, bouncing and glinting eerily as the van approached the grave. It was backed to the open ground. Workers opened the back door. Ruffian had been covered in a white canvas shroud. Workers removed her body carefully from the van and cradled it to the bottom of the grave. The lights of other vehicles shone on the scene.

No one said anything until Whiteley handed the coolers to Mike Bell and said, "You put them on her." Bell climbed into the grave, covered her with the blankets and climbed back out again. Wordlessly, then, everybody turned and left.

Workers began to fill the grave with dirt. The lights went out. Stable hands sank back into the darkness of the barns. All that was left were the memories. Only the legend lived.

. . . . . . . . . . . . . . . . .

There is one final thing. The next night, I was at the Nassau Coliseum to cover Billy Jean's triumphant return from Wimbledon, where she had just won her sixth Wimbledon singles title. The events of the last two days had left me feeling a numbness unto death. I had been a zombie through it all, even as I stood before Ruffian as she went into shock in her stall, even as it grew dark around the grave, even as Mike Bell went down to cover her and I could hear a soft weeping in the dark of the barns beyond the bowl of gravesite light. I was at the press table in the Coliseum when they played the national anthem. We all rose from our seats. The place went totally dark.

They shined a spotlight on the flag. The lights played on the wall. They were the headlights coming at me on the infield of the night before. There was the freshly opened grave. There she was covered in the white canvas shroud. There she was in a panic by the backstretch hedge and Gilman was holding up her leg and he had blood all over his hands. There she was trying to lie down in that stall as men fought to keep her on her feet and the ice water had turned red and the foot was dangling above it and her large brown eyes were rimmed in white ... They were playing the national anthem and the lights kept playing on the grave and I started choking on myself with my hands over my eyes and weeping and the reporter standing next to me turned and said, Jeez, what's wrong with you? What happened? Are you okay?

I am fine, I said, I'm fine. Just a bad time. I'll be all right.

# ACKNOWLEDGMENTS

. . . . . . . . . . . . . . . . .

During the course of Ruffian's extraordinary two-year career, I had the good fortune of being not only the regular turfwriter for *Newsday*, the Long Island paper, but also the New York correspondent for *The Thoroughbred Record* out of Lexington, Kentucky, then one of two major weekly magazines devoted to covering the American thoroughbred breeding and racing industry. That I had two outlets for my turfwriting in those days was, as things turned out, extremely fortunate for me. I covered nine of Ruffian's eleven lifetime starts, including her only adventure outside of New York—in the Sorority Stakes at Monmouth Park, on the New Jersey shore—and I was able to return to the scenes of all her surpassing performances by revisiting those two primary sources: my old *Newsday* stories, as entombed in the Library of Congress, in Washington, D.C., and my *Thoroughbred Record* pieces, as preserved at the Keeneland Library in Lexington, the greatest repository of racing books and periodicals in America. Of course, space was far more limited in *Newsday* than in the magazine, and what I could not get into my *Newsday* stories, for lack of elbow room, I always managed to slip into my dispatches to *The Thoroughbred Record*. What I ended up with, as I peeled back this onion more than thirty years later, was a kind of diary of Ruffian's life as seen through my own eyes and the eyes of those I had interviewed at the time—from race to race and winner's circle to winner's circle, from her life as a two-year-old phenom to her burial in the infield at Belmont Park.

Looking back, I see that I owe a vast debt of thanks to Dave Laventhol, the editor of *Newsday*, for turning me from a political/environmental writer to a chronicler of the turf; to former *Newsday* sports editor Stan Isaacs, for encouraging me as I began covering racing and sports; to *Newsday* sports editor Dick Sandler, for demanding more, even insisting on more, in the reporting and the writing; and to Arnold Kirkpatrick, my editor at *The Thoroughbred Record*, for hiring and trusting me as his magazine's voice in New York, particularly during Ruffian's heyday in the sport.

I also want to thank the staff at the Library of Congress, that most glorious and unsung of federal institutions, for fetching up all those ancient newspaper stories and making my research so easy for so many years. And lastly, I want to thank especially the staff at the Keeneland Library, particularly Phyllis Rogers and Cathy Schenck, for their generous help and cooperation in my hours spent reading, working and researching there.

# PHOTOGRAPHY AND ILLUSTRATION CREDITS

. . . . . . . . . . . . . . . . .